# DISNEY
# ZOOTOPIA

Adapted by Suzanne Francis

The wild sounds of **ancient predators echo**ed through a large **barn** in Bunnyburrow. A young bunny named Judy Hopps appeared on a **makeshift** stage, trying to find her way through a papier-mâché* and cardboard* jungle.

Judy's voice rang out loud and clear. "Fear. **Treachery. Bloodlust!** Thousands of years ago, these were the **forces** that ruled our world. A world where **prey** were **scared** of predators. And predators had an **uncontrollable** desire to **maim** and **maul** and—"

---

★papier-mâché 파피에 마셰. 펄프에 아교를 섞어 만든 종이 반죽으로 습기에 무르고 마르면 매우 단단해진다.
✳cardboard 판지. 기계로 눌러서 만든 두꺼운 종이.

Suddenly, a jaguar* **leapt** on her from the shadows!

"Blood, blood, blood!" Judy screamed as she **crumpled** under the attack. "And death."

After a long and **drawn-out** moment of terrible silence, Judy sat up, faced the **confused** audience, and smiled as she continued her **monologue**. A **banner** reading CARROT DAYS TALENT SHOW hung over the **stun**ned crowd.

"Back then, the world was divided in two: **vicious** predator or **meek** prey." Two cardboard boxes dropped down from the ceiling. The first, **label**ed VICIOUS PREDATOR in crayon, **land**ed on top of the jaguar, and the second, labeled MEEK PREY, landed on Judy. The boxes **settled** on their shoulders so their heads, arms, and legs stuck out. "But over time, we **evolved** and moved beyond our **primitive, savage** ways."

A young sheep wearing a white **robe** and a cardboard rainbow on his head did an **improvisation**al dance across the stage. Judy and the jaguar **burst** out of their boxes, now wearing white robes, too. "Now predator and prey live in

---

★jaguar 재규어. 아메리카 대륙에서 가장 큰 고양잇과 맹수로, 몸의 빛깔은 회색 또는 황갈색이며 검은색 테두리 안에 점이 박힌 무늬가 있다.

harmony."

Judy and the jaguar, **reveal**ed as another **friendly youngster**, shook hands as the sheep **sprinkled glitter** on them. "And every young **mammal** has **multitudinous** opportunities," Judy said.

"Yeah. I don't have to **cower** in a **herd** anymore," said the sheep. Then he **rip**ped off his robe, revealing a homemade **astronaut costume**. "Instead, I can be an astronaut."

"I don't have to grow up to be a lonely hunter," said the jaguar, showing a business suit under his robe. "Today I can hunt for **tax exempt**ions. I'm gonna be an **actuary**!"

"And no longer do I have to **blind**ly **serve** the **almighty** carrot," said Judy. "I can make the world a better place— saving lives, **defend**ing the **defenseless**! I am going to be . . ." Judy ripped off her robe and stood in a blue **uniform**. "A police **officer**!"

In the audience, a **nasty** fox kid named Gideon Grey **snicker**ed to his two friends. "Bunny **cop**. That is the most stupidest thing I ever heard," he said.

Back **onstage**, it was almost as if Judy had heard his **remark**. "It may seem impossible . . . to small minds," she

said, pointing at him. "I'm looking at you, Gideon Grey."
Judy **snap**ped her fingers and a **backdrop** showing a bright
city **skyline** unrolled behind her. "But just two hundred and
eleven miles* away stands the great city of . . . ZOOTOPIA!
Where our **ancestors** first joined together in peace. And
**declare**d that Anyone Can Be Anything! Thank you and
good night!"

Judy proudly **bow**ed, as if she had just given the
performance of her life. **Dutiful applause** came from the
audience, **including** her parents, Bonnie and Stu Hopps.

Moments later, Judy, still wearing her police costume,
excitedly exited the barn with her parents. Outside, the
Carrot Days Festival **was in full swing** as everyone enjoyed
**booth**s, games, and **rides**.

"Judy, ever wonder how your mom and me got to be so
darn* happy?" Stu asked.

"Nope," Judy answered.

"Well, I'll tell ya how," Stu continued, as if he hadn't
heard Judy. "We **gave up** on our dreams and we settled,

---

★ mile 거리의 단위인 마일. 1마일은 약 1,609미터이다.
✳ darn '젠장', '제기랄'이라는 뜻의 'damn'을 완곡하게 표현한 말.

right, Bon?"

"Oh yes," Bonnie agreed. "That's right, Stu. We settled hard."

"See, that's the beauty of **complacency**, Jude. If you don't try anything new, you'll never fail," Stu said.

"I like trying, actually," Judy said.

Bonnie looked at their daughter. "What your father means, hon . . . it's gonna be difficult—impossible, even— for you to become a police officer."

"There's never been a bunny cop," Stu said.

"I guess I'll have to be the first one!" said Judy as she parkoured★ against a fence. "Because I'm gonna make the world a better place."

"Or . . . heck,✲ you wanna talk about making the world a better place—no better way to do it than becoming a carrot farmer," said Stu.

"Yes! Your dad and me and your two hundred seventy-five brothers and sisters—we're changing the world one carrot at a time," said Bonnie.

---

★parkour 파쿠르. 도심의 구조물을 오르고 뛰어다니는 스포츠로, 여기에서는 동사로 쓰였다.
✲heck '제기랄', '빌어먹을'이라는 뜻의 'hell'을 완곡하게 표현한 말.

"**Amen to that.** Carrot farming is a **noble profession**," Stu agreed.

But Judy stopped paying attention to her parents when she **spot**ted Gideon Grey following some little kids. She was **instant**ly **alert**, and she went after him.

"You get it, honey?" Bonnie asked Judy. "I mean, it's great to have dreams."

"Yeah, just as long as you don't believe in them too much," Stu continued as he looked around for his daughter. "Jude? Where the heck did she go?"

Judy got closer and saw Gideon Grey doing what the fox did best—**bully**ing some kids.

"Give me your tickets right now, or I'm gonna kick your **meek** little sheep **butt**," said Gideon, before giving the kid a **shove**. Then he took the sheep's tickets and **smack**ed her with them. "Baa-baa," he **mock**ed. "What're ya gonna do, cry?"

"Ow!" **yelp**ed the sheep. "**Cut it out**, Gideon!"

"Hey!" said Judy firmly. "You heard her. Cut it out."

Gideon looked at Judy and laughed. "Nice **costume**, **loser**," he **snarl**ed. "What crazy world are you living in where you think a bunny could be a **cop**?"

"Kindly return my friend's tickets," Judy said calmly.

Gideon snarled and **stuff**ed the tickets into his pocket. "Come get 'em. But **watch out**, 'cause I'm a fox. And like you said in your **dumb** little stage play, us **predators** used to eat **prey**. And that killer **instinct** is still in our Dunnahh."

"I'm pretty sure it's **pronounced** D-N-A," **whispered** one of Gideon's wolf **pals**.

"Don't tell me what I know, Travis," Gideon said, **irritated**.

"You don't **scare** me, Gideon," said Judy.

Gideon shoved Judy so hard that she fell to the ground with a **thud**. Judy's eyes began to water.

"You scared now?" Gideon said **cruel**ly. The other prey animals **cower**ed behind a tree, leaving Judy to face the bullies alone.

"Look at her nose **twitch**," said Travis **mocking**ly. "She *is* scared!"

"Cry, little baby bunny. Cry, cry—" Gideon **taunt**ed.

*Bam!* Before Gideon could say another word, Judy kicked him in the face with her **hind** legs, **knock**ing him down. But he **sprang** right back up, and he was mad.

"Oh, you don't know when to quit, do you?" Gideon said, **unsheathing** his **claw**s like a **fist** of knives.

He **slap**ped Judy in the face, his sharp claws **dig**ging into her skin, making her **bleed**. Then he knocked her down and held her face in the dirt. "I want you to remember this moment," Gideon said coldly, "anytime you think you'll ever be anything more than just a stupid, carrot-farming dumb bunny."

Gideon and his pals walked away, laughing, leaving Judy in the dirt. She got up, **wipe**d the blood off her **cheek**, and **glare**d at their backs.

"Aw jeez,★ that looks bad," said Gareth, a sheep.

"Are you okay, Judy?" asked Sharla, the sheep the bullies had taken the tickets from.

Judy took a breath and pulled something out of her front pocket, smiling wide.

"Here you go!" she said, returning the tickets that Gideon had stolen.

"**Wicked**! You got our tickets!" said Sharla.

---

★jeez '이런', '어머나'라는 뜻으로 화, 놀람 등을 나타낸다. 'Jesus(예수)'에서 유래했다.

"You're **awesome**, Judy!" **exclaim**ed Gareth.

"That Gideon Grey doesn't know what he's talking about," Sharla added.

Judy slapped her police hat back on top of her head, and there was a look of **determination** in her eye. "Well, he was right about one thing: I don't know when to quit."

**F**ifteen years later, Judy Hopps **worked her tail off** in the Zootopia Police Academy. She was small compared to the rest of the **cadet**s—who were mostly elephants, rhinos,* and bison*—but she was **strong-willed**.

Because of her size, the **physical** training was the toughest part. Cadets had to **get through obstacle**s in **simulator**s that **mimic**ked all of the twelve **unique ecosystem**s that **made up** the city of Zootopia. From **freezing** Tundratown*

---

★ rhino (= rhinoceros) 코뿔소. 머리에 1개 또는 2개의 뿔이 있으며, 피부가 두껍고 각질화된 것이 특징이다.

✳ bison 들소. 등에 척추가 자란 혹이 나 있는 것이 특징이다.

✻ tundra 툰드라. 북극해 연안에 분포하는 넓은 벌판. 연중 대부분은 눈과 얼음으로 덮여 있으나 짧은 여름 동안에 지표의 일부가 녹아서 이끼가 자란다.

to **sweltering** Sahara\* **Square,** each ecosystem presented its own set of challenges—whether it was trying to **scale** an ice wall or survive in a **scorching sandstorm.**

Judy fell down more than anyone. In her mind she could hear the voices of her parents, her **drill instructor,** and Gideon Grey all **doubt**ing that there could ever be a bunny cop. And it was those voices that made Judy work harder than anyone else. Through **persistence** and **perseverance,** she managed to **keep up** and surprise everyone.

In the final weeks of training, Judy used her bunny skills, like her strong legs and her great hearing, to help prove her worth. She **sailed through** the physical obstacles and at times even passed the other cadets. Once, she **knock**ed down a male rhino ten times her size during a final **spar**ring session!

On **graduation** day, Judy took her place among the other graduates during the ceremony, **including** the rhino who **sport**ed a **fat lip** and a **black eye.** The **mayor,** a lion named Leodore Lionheart, stepped up to the **podium.**

---

★Sahara 사하라 사막. 아프리카 북부, 대서양 연안에서 나일 강 유역에 걸친 세계 최대의 사막.

"As mayor of Zootopia, I am proud to **announce** that my **Mammal** Inclusion **Initiative**★ has produced its first police academy graduate. The **valedictorian** of her class . . . ZPD's✻ very first rabbit police **officer**, Judy Hopps. **Assistant** Mayor Bellwether, her **badge**?" the mayor said to a small sheep standing nearby.

"Oh! Yes. Right," said Bellwether.

"Judy, it is my great **privilege** to officially **assign** you to the heart of Zootopia: **Precinct** One, City Center," Lionheart said.

Judy walked across the stage to the sound of **deafening applause**—the loudest coming from her parents, even as Stu **sob**bed.

Mayor Lionheart handed Judy her **diploma** while Bellwether stepped forward and **pin**ned her ZPD badge onto her **uniform**. "**Congratulations**, Officer Hopps."

"I won't **let** you **down**. This has been my dream since I was a kid," said Judy.

---

★Mammal Inclusion Initiative 포유동물 통합 계획. 모든 포유동물은 종과 크기에 상관 없이 공평한 대우를 받아야 한다는 정책으로, 인간 세상의 '소수 민족·인종 포용 정책'과 비슷한 개념이다.
✻ZPD 주토피아 시 경찰국. Zootopia Police Department의 약자.

"It's a real proud day for us little guys," Bellwether **whispered**.

"Bellwether, **make room**, will you?" said Lionheart, smiling broadly. "All right, Officer Hopps. Let's see those teeth!"

A photographer posed Judy with Mayor Lionheart and Bellwether. But Lionheart **edged** Bellwether out of the photo.

Days later, Judy's parents, along with several **siblings**, **accompanied** her to the train station.

"We're real proud of you, Judy," said Bonnie.

"Yeah. Scared, too," said Stu. "Really, it's a proud-scared combo. I mean, Zootopia. It's so far away and such a big city."

"Guys, I've been working for this my whole life," Judy told her parents, trying to hide how **thrill**ed she really was.

"We know," said Bonnie. "And we're just a little excited for you, but **terrified**."

"'The only thing we have to fear is fear itself,'" said Judy.

"And also bears," said Stu. "We have bears to fear, too. **To say nothing of** lions, wolves . . ."

"Wolves?" Bonnie asked, **perplex**ed.

". . . weasels . . . ,*" Stu continued.

"You play cribbage* with a weasel," said Bonnie.

"And he **cheat**s like there's no tomorrow. Pretty much all predators do—and Zootopia's full of 'em. And foxes are the worst."

"Actually, your father does have a point there," added Bonnie. "It's in their **biology.** Remember what happened with Gideon Grey?"

"When I was nine," said Judy. "Gideon Grey was a **jerk** who happened to be a fox. I know plenty of bunnies who are jerks."

"Sure. We all do. Absolutely," said Stu. "But just **in case,** we made you a little **care package** to take with you." He held out a bag.

"And I put some snacks in there," said Bonnie.

---

★ weasel 족제비. 주둥이가 뾰족하며 다리는 짧고 네 다리의 발가락 사이에는 물갈퀴가 있다. 움직임이 재빠르고 후각과 청각이 발달하였다.

✳ cribbage 크리비지. 두 명 이상이 할 수 있는 카드 게임. 크리비지 판 위에 페그를 움직여 점수를 기록한다.

Judy looked inside and saw a **bunch** of pink **spray canister**s.

"This is fox **repellent**," explained Stu, picking one up.

"Yeah, that's safe to have," said Bonnie.

"This is fox **deterrent** . . . ," Stu said, pointing at something that looked like an air **horn**.*

"The deterrent and the repellent. That's all she needs," Bonnie said, trying to stop Stu from **going overboard**.

"**Check** this **out**!" Stu said as he pulled out a fox Taser* and turned it on, causing it to **sizzle**.

"Oh, for **goodness**' sake! She has no need for a fox Taser, Stu."

"Come on. When is there not a need for a fox Taser?" asked Stu.

"Okay, I will take this to make you stop talking," said Judy. She **grab**bed the pink can of fox repellent as the train approached.

"**Terrific**! Everyone wins!" Stu **exclaim**ed.

---

★ air horn 압축 공기로 진동판을 진동시켜 소리를 내는 경적으로, 스포츠 경기의 시작을 알릴 때 등에 사용한다.

✵ Taser 전기 충격기. Taser International에서 판매하는 작은 쇠화살을 쏘아 전기 충격을 가하는 무기.

"Arriving! Zootopia express!" called the **conductor**.

"Okay. Gotta go. Bye!" said Judy, heading for the train.

Stu and Bonnie **held back** tears as they watched their daughter walk off. Suddenly, Judy turned back and ran to her parents. She **wrap**ped her arms around them both. "I love you guys," she said, hugging them.

"Love you, too!" said Bonnie.

After one more hug, Judy jumped onto the train.

"Cripes,★ here come the **waterworks**," said Stu as his tears started to **flow**. *"Ahhahoho jeesh . . ."*

"Oh, Stu, **pull** it **together**," whispered Bonnie.

The big crowd of bunnies watched Judy go, and as the train **pull**ed **away**, they ran next to it, **waving** and shouting their goodbyes.

"Bye, everybody! Bye!" Judy called.

When their faces **faded** into the **distance**, Judy climbed to the **observation deck** and took a deep breath. She pulled out her phone and **click**ed on some music, feeling like her life was about to begin.

---

★ cripes 놀람 또는 짜증을 나타내는 표현으로 '에이!', '저런!'이라는 뜻이다.

**A**s the train came around a **bend**, Judy **gaze**d out the window at the **incredible sight** in the **distance:** Zootopia. She **press**ed her face against the glass and watched each **borough** of the city pass by.

Judy exited the train at Central Station, which **served downtown** Zootopia, and **made her way** outside into the city's central plaza. It was incredible! She took out her **earbud**s and let the **chaotic** city sounds **wash over** her as she looked around, **awestruck.** Animals of all shapes and sizes **rush**ed by, hurrying this way and that. It **was a far cry from** Bunnyburrow!

She looked down at her phone and checked her maps

app* to **figure out** which way to go.

When she found her apartment building, the **landlady**, Dharma, an armadillo,* led her to a little apartment.

"Welcome to the Grand Pangolin* Arms," said Dharma, stepping aside to **let** Judy **in**. "**Complimentary delousing** once a month. Don't lose your key."

Kudu and Oryx, Judy's **neighbor**s, passed in the **hallway**. Judy **greet**ed them warmly. "Oh, hi, I'm Judy. Your new neighbor."

"Yeah, well, we're loud," said Kudu.

"Don't expect us to **apologize** for it," added Oryx.

The two hurried off, **slam**ming the door of their apartment behind them. Dharma had left as well, leaving Judy alone in her apartment for the first time. She looked around.

"**Greasy** walls . . . **rickety** bed . . . ," said Judy.

Then loud voices came from the other side of the wall:

---

★app 앱. 스마트 폰 등에 내려받아 사용할 수 있는 응용프로그램. '애플리케이션(application)'을 줄인 말이다.
✻armadillo 아르마딜로. 북미 남부에서 남미에 걸쳐 볼 수 있는 야행성 동물. 등이 갑옷 모양의 단단한 딱지로 덮여 있어서 적을 만나면 몸을 둥글게 말아 몸을 지킨다.
✳pangolin 천산갑. 몸의 위쪽이 딱딱한 비늘로 덮여 있고, 긴 혀로 곤충을 핥아먹는 작은 동물.

"Shut up!" "You shut up!" "No! You shut up!"

"Crazy neighbors." Judy **flop**ped onto the bed with a big smile. "I *love* it!"

*Beep. Beep. Beep.* At the sound of her morning **alarm**, Judy **sprang** out of bed. She washed, brushed, and **rinse**d. Then she put on her **vest**, **pin**ned on her **badge**, and **strap**ped on her belt. She was ready to protect the city! She **glance**d at the pink can of fox **repellent** sitting on the bedside table and walked out, leaving it behind. But after a moment, she reached back in the room and **grab**bed it—just **in case**.

She left her apartment and headed toward the Zootopia Police Department for her first day on the job!

Judy's eyes **widen**ed as she entered the **chaotic** and loud ZPD. Big **burly** cops pushed **criminal**s through the lobby as people **rush**ed around in every direction. She **dodge**d a few **husky** animals before finally finding her way to the front desk. There, a **pudgy, friendly**-looking cheetah* sat **chat**ting with some other cops. Judy smiled at him as she approached, but he couldn't see her because she was shorter than the desk.

"Excuse me!" Judy called up to the desk. "Down here. Down. *Here.* Hi."

The cheetah **lean**ed over the desk and saw Judy standing there in her uniform.

"O-M **goodness**!" he said. "They really did **hire** a bunny. What! I gotta tell you; you are even cuter than I thought you'd be."

Judy **winced**. "Oh, uh, I'm sure you didn't know, but for us rabbits . . . the word 'cute' is a—it's a little—"

"Oh! I am so sorry. *Me*, Benjamin Clawhauser, the guy everyone thinks is just a **flabby**, donut-loving cop, **stereotyping** *you* . . . ," he said **apologetic**ally.

"It's okay. Oh, um, actually you've—actually—" Judy **stammer**ed as she tried to **figure out** how to say it. "There's a—in your neck—the **fold** . . . there's—"

---

★cheetah 치타. 고양이과의 포유류로 얼굴에 검은색 줄무늬가 있다. 포유류 중에서 가장 **빠른** 동물로 최고 시속이 110킬로미터 전후이다.

Clawhauser removed a small donut from under a roll of neck fat. "There you went, you little dickens!*" said Clawhauser to the donut. Then he **joyfully cram**med it into his mouth.

"I should get to **roll call**, so . . . which way do I . . . ?" Judy asked.

"Oh!" Clawhauser said with his mouth full of donut. "Bullpen's* over there to the left."

"Great, thank you!" Judy said, and hurried off.

"Aw . . . that poor little bunny's gonna get eaten alive," he said, watching her go.

Inside the bullpen, rhinos, buffalo,* hippos,* and elephants prepared for work. They **tower**ed over Judy, but she didn't mind. She excitedly climbed up into a **massive**, elephant-sized chair and **gaze**d around the room.

"Hey. Officer Hopps," Judy **extend**ed her **paw** to a **gigantic** rhino whose name **tag** read MCHORN. "You ready

---

★ dickens '악마(devil)'를 완곡하게 표현한 말로 여기에서는 '개구쟁이'라는 뜻의 속어로 사용되었다.
✳ bullpen 불펜. 원래는 야구장에서 투수가 경기 중에 연습이나 운동을 하는 장소이지만, 여기에서는 개별 공간을 벽으로 막지 않은 넓은 사무실을 의미한다.
✲ buffalo 물소. 뿔이 무겁고 길며 뒤로 젖혀져 있는 것이 특징이다.
✳ hippo (= hippopotamus) 하마. 코끼리와 코뿔소 다음으로 체격이 큰 동물이다. 강, 호수, 연못 등지에서 서식하고 물에서 생활하는 시간이 많지만, 수영은 잘하지 못한다.

to make the world a better place?" she asked **sincerely**.

McHorn **snort**ed and **reluctant**ly gave her a **fist bump**,* nearly knocking her off her chair.

"TEN-HUT!*" shouted one of the officers as Police **Chief** Bogo, a **gruff** Cape buffalo,* entered the room. Everyone **instant**ly **fell in line** and started **stomp**ing on the floor.

"All right, all right. Everybody sit," said Bogo. "I've got three items on the **docket**. First, we need to **acknowledge** the elephant in the room.*" He **nod**ded toward an elephant officer. "Francine, happy birthday."

The shy elephant **blush**ed as the cops **clap**ped, snorted, and **hoot**ed. "Number two: there are some new **recruit**s with us I should introduce. But I'm not going to, because I don't care."

Bogo moved toward a map. "Finally, we have fourteen missing mammal cases," he said, **gesturing** to the **pushpin-**

---

★fist bump 주먹끼리 툭 부딪치는 인사.

✴ten-hut 군대나 경찰에서 쓰는 용어로 '차렷!'이라는 뜻이다.

✳Cape buffalo 아프리카 물소. 크고 검은색을 띠는 물소로 이마 위로 자란 뿔이 마치 헬멧과 같은 모습을 하고 있다.

✴the elephant in the room 모두가 알고 있으면서 애써 모르는 척하는 커다란 문제를 나타내는 표현. 하지만 여기에서는 실제 코끼리를 가리키면서 재미를 주고 있다.

covered map. "FOURTEEN CASES. Now, that's more than we've ever had, and City Hall is right up my **tail** to solve them. This is **priority** one. **Assign**ments!"

Bogo began **bark**ing out assignments as one of the officers handed out case files. "Officers Grizzoli, Fangmeyer, Delgato: your teams take missing mammals from the Rainforest* **District**. Officers McHorn, Rhinowitz, Wolfard: your teams take Sahara **Square**. Officers Higgins, Snarlov, Trunkaby: Tundratown. And finally, our first bunny, Officer Hopps."

Judy sat up, she'd been waiting **anxious**ly for her assignment. Bogo grabbed the last case file from Higgins and held it **dramatic**ally in the air as he looked at Judy.

"Parking duty. **Dismiss**ed!"

"Parking duty?" asked Judy quietly. She hurried after Bogo. "Uh, Chief? Chief Bogo?"

Bogo looked around and saw no one until he looked down to see Judy at his **ankle**s.

"Sir, you said there are fourteen missing mammal cases."

★rainforest 우림(雨林). 연중 우량이 많고 습윤하게 유지되며 수목의 생육이 좋고 울창한 밀림이 조성된 숲.

"So?"

"So I can handle one. You probably forgot, but I was top of my class at the academy."

"Didn't forget. Just don't care."

"Sir, I'm not just some **token** bunny."

"Well, then writing a hundred tickets★ a day should be easy," said Bogo, walking out and **slam**ming the door behind him.

"A hundred tickets," said Judy, stomping her foot. She turned toward the closed door and shouted, "I'm gonna write *two hundred* tickets! Before noon!"

---

★ticket 교통 법규 위반에 대한 벌금을 부과하는 딱지.

**S**porting her **traffic-enforcement** hat and a bright-orange **vest**, Judy climbed into her parking cart, **buckled** up, and put on her **shades**. She **pressed** the gas pedal down and **took off** . . . very slowly.

Judy's ears **twisted** and turned as she used her excellent hearing skills to listen for **expired** parking meters.★ Each time one **dinged**, she **dashed** over and wrote a ticket. She ticketed **dozens** of cars of every size—moose✳ cars, mouse cars, and everything in between.

"**Boom**! Two hundred tickets before noon," she said

---

★ parking meter 주차장의 주차 요금 징수기.
✳ moose 무스. 현존하는 가장 큰 사슴으로, 몸집이 말보다 크다.

proudly.

She turned to see her traffic cart parked at an expired meter. "Two hundred and *one*," she said with a **self-satisfied** smile as she wrote *herself* a ticket.

Then the sound of a car **horn** and an angry sheep **yell**ing out his window **interrupt**ed her moment. "Watch where you're going, fox!" the sheep yelled.

Judy saw a red fox across the street and eyed him **suspicious**ly. Then she shook her head and **scold**ed herself for being suspicious without a real reason. But when she saw him look around before **slink**ing into Jumbeaux's Café, she crossed the road and **peek**ed in through the window. He was nowhere to be seen.

Now completely suspicious, Judy **unsnapp**ed the pink can of fox repellent from her **holster** and headed inside.

The café was an elephant ice cream **parlor**. Elephants used their **trunks** to **scoop** ice cream into bowls and decorate sundaes* with nuts, **whipp**ed cream,* and cherries. Judy

---

★ sundae 아이스크림선디. 긴 유리잔에 아이스크림을 넣고 그 위에 시럽, 견과류, 과일 조각 등을 얹은 것을 말한다.
✷ whipped cream 휘핑크림. 생크림에 거품이 일게 한 것으로 과자의 장식에 쓰이거나 그대로 커피에 넣기도 한다.

spotted the fox at the front of the line. Jerry Jumbeaux, Jr., the elephant working behind the counter, yelled at the fox. "Listen, I don't know what you're doing skulking around during daylight hours, but I don't want any trouble here. So hit the road!"

"I'm not looking for any trouble either, sir, I simply want to buy a Jumbo-pop," said the fox innocently, reaching behind him, "for my little boy. You want the red or the blue, pal?"

When Judy noticed the little toddler clinging to the fox's leg, she felt awful for jumping to conclusions. "I'm such a . . . ," Judy muttered to herself as she turned to leave.

"Listen, buddy. There aren't any fox ice cream joints in your part of town?"

"There are. It's just, my boy—" The fox tousled the boy's fur. "This goofy little stinker*—he loves all things elephant. Wants to be one when he grows up. Who the heck am I to crush the little guy's dreams?"

The boy pulled up the hood of his elephant costume

---

★stinker 원래는 '골칫거리' 또는 '불쾌한 놈'이라는 뜻이지만 여기에서는 '개구쟁이'라는 애칭으로 쓰였다.

and made a cute little *toot-toot* sound with his toy elephant trunk. Judy smiled. Realizing she still had it out, she quickly tucked her fox repellent back into its holster.

"Look, you probably can't read, fox, but the **sign** says"—Jerry pointed to the sign as he read it slowly— "WE **RESERVE** THE RIGHT TO REFUSE SERVICE TO ANYONE. So **beat it**."

"You're **hold**ing **up** the line," said an **annoyed** elephant, waiting behind them.

The little toddler looked as if he was about to cry. Judy **march**ed up to the counter and **flash**ed her badge at Jerry.

"Hello? Excuse me?" said Judy.

"You're gonna have to wait your turn like everyone else, meter maid,*" said Jerry.

"Actually . . . I'm an officer. Just had a quick question. Are your **customer**s aware that they're getting **snot** and **mucus** with their cookies and cream?"

"What are you talking about?" asked Jerry, annoyed.

"Well, I don't want to cause you any trouble, but I

---

★meter maid 주차 위반 단속 여자 경찰관.

believe scooping ice cream with an ungloved trunk is a class-three health-code violation. Which is kind of a big deal. Of course, I could let you off with a warning if you were to glove those trunks and—I don't know—finish selling this nice dad and his son a . . . what was it?" Judy smiled at the fox.

"A Jumbo-pop," said the fox.

"A Jumbo-pop," said Judy firmly.

Jerry stared for a moment, then said, "Fifteen dollars."

The fox turned to Judy. "Thank you so much. Thank you." He dug through his pockets before stopping in disbelief. "Are you kidding me? I don't have my wallet. I'm sorry, pal, worst birthday ever." The fox leaned down to give the toddler a kiss, then turned to Judy. "Thanks anyway."

Judy slapped some cash on the counter. "Keep the change," she said.

Once Jerry gave them the Jumbo-pop, Judy held the door as the fox and his little boy exited Jumbeaux's.

"Officer, I can't thank you enough," said the fox. "So kind, really. Can I pay you back?"

"Oh no, my treat. It just—you know, it burns me up to

see **folks** with such backward attitudes toward foxes," Judy said. "Well, I just wanna say, you're a great dad and just a . . . a real **articulate fellow.**"

"Ah, well, that is high praise. It's **rare** that I find someone so non-**patronizing** . . . Officer . . ."

"Hopps. Mr. . . . ," Judy said, not catching the **sarcasm** that was **evident** in the fox's **tone.**

"Wilde. Nick Wilde."

Judy **bent** down toward the little fox. "And you, little guy, you want to be an elephant when you grow up . . . you be an elephant—because this is Zootopia, and anyone can be anything." She placed a ZPD badge sticker on the boy's chest.

"All right, here you go—" Nick said, handing him the huge Jumbo-pop. "Two **paws.** Yeah. Aw, look at that smile, that's a happy birthday smile! Give her a little bye-bye toot-toot."

The **adorable** little fox tooted his trunk.

"Toot-toot!" said Judy happily. Then she walked off with **a spring in her step.** It felt great to help somebody in need!

**A** little while later, Judy was writing parking tickets in Sahara Square when she **notice**d Nick and his kid a few **block**s away. "Oh! Hey, little **toot**-toot!" she called, **waving**, but they didn't see her.

She started toward them but stopped suddenly when she realized what they were doing. They were *melting* the giant Jumbo-pop she had bought for them in the hot sun. Then they were **channel**ing the juice into little **jug**s. Judy **furrow**ed her **brow** as she watched Nick and his kid packing the full jugs into the back of a **van**. Her eyes nearly fell out of her head when she saw Nick's little son get into the driver's seat! Then they drove off. Judy was shocked and confused.

She **hop**ped in her cart and followed them to the coldest **section** of Zootopia—Tundratown. Nick's son was using his little paws to make **mold**s in the snow, which Nick then put sticks in. Then the two **pour**ed the juice from the melted Jumbo-pop into the molds to create **dozen**s of smaller pops! Judy looked on, **scandalized**. She couldn't believe it!

Judy followed them again, this time to Savanna Central, where they **set up** a **stand** and sold "pawpsicles"★ at **mark**ed-**up** prices to lemmings.✳

"Pawpsicles! Get your pawpsicles!" **bark**ed Nick.

One lemming bought an icy **treat**, and then the rest of them followed. In an **instant**, the **frozen dessert**s were completely sold out! Once the lemmings finished their pawpsicles, they threw the sticks into a **recycling bin**. When the lemmings were gone, a small door opened in the bin and the little fox—who, Judy realized, was *not* an **adorable**

---

★ pawpsicle 발(paw)모양 아이스캔디(popsicle). 본래 상표명이었지만 지금은 '아이스캔디'라는 뜻
의 보통 명사로 쓰이는 'popsicle'이라는 단어에 'paw(발)'를 붙여 재치 있게 사용하고 있다.
✳ lemming 레밍. 몇 년마다 크게 증식하여 이동하므로 나그네쥐라고도 한다. 주로 산악지대나 툰
드라, 황야에 서식하며, 집단을 이루어 생활한다.

**toddler** but a *fully grown* Fennec fox* named Finnick—stepped out with a **bundle** of used pawpsicle sticks. Judy was having trouble believing her eyes.

She continued to follow Nick and Finnick to Little Rodentia, where Nick **plop**ped down the bundle of used sticks in front of a mouse **construction** worker and shouted, "**Lumber** delivery!"

"What's with the color?" asked the construction worker.

"The color? It's *red* wood," answered Nick, **shrug**ging **off** the question as he accepted his payment.

The construction workers **haul**ed the sticks away, and Judy watched in **awe** as Nick handed Finnick his share of the cash.

"Thirty-nine . . . forty. There you go. Way to work that **diaper**, big guy. What, no kiss bye-bye for Daddy?" Nick asked **jokingly**.

"You kiss me tomorrow, I'll **bite** your face off," said Finnick in a deep voice. "*Ciao.*" Finnick hopped into his van and drove off, **blaring** loud rap music.

---

★Fennec fox 사막여우. 체구에 비해 귀가 엄청나게 크고 길다. 발바닥에도 털이 나 있어서 사막에서도 모래에 빠지지 않고 걸어다닐 수 있다.

Judy appeared in front of Nick, her face burning with anger. "I **stood up for** you. And you lied to me! You *liar!*" she **yelled**.

"It's called a **hustle, sweetheart**," said Nick coolly. "And I'm not the liar, he is." Nick pointed behind Judy. She turned but saw no one standing there. When she **whip**ped back around, Nick was gone! Then she spotted his **tail** disappearing behind a corner.

"Hey," she said, hurrying to **catch up** as Nick **stroll**ed along. "All right, **slick** Nick, you're under **arrest**."

"Really, for what?"

"**Gee**, I don't know. How about selling food without a **permit, transport**ing undeclared **commerce** across **borough** lines, false **advertising**—"

"Permit." Nick smiled as he showed Judy the document. "**Receipt** of declared commerce." He showed her a receipt. "And I did not falsely advertise anything. Take care."

"You told that mouse the pawpsicle sticks were redwood," Judy said.

"That's right," said Nick **smug**ly. "Red. Wood. With a space in the middle. Wood that is red. You can't touch me,

Carrots. I've been doing this since I was born."

"You're gonna want to **refrain** from calling me Carrots."

"My bad," said Nick. "I just naturally **assume**d you came from some little carrot-**choke**d Podunk, no?"

"Ah, no," Judy replied, as if to say "obviously not." "Podunk is in Deerbrooke **County**. I grew up in Bunnyburrow."

"Okay. Tell me if this story sounds familiar." Nick's **tone** changed as he began to talk quickly and **bold**ly. "**Naïve** little **hick** with good grades and big ideas decides, 'Hey, look at me, I'm gonna move to Zootopia, where **predator**s and **prey** live in **harmony** and sing "Kumbaya"*!' Only to find—whoopsie,* we don't all **get along**. And that dream of being a big-city **cop**? Double whoopsie! She's a meter maid. And whoopsie number threesie, *no one* cares about her or her dreams. Soon enough those dreams die and our bunny sinks into **emotional** and **literal squalor**, living in a box under a bridge. Until, finally, she has no choice but to go back home with that cute fuzzy wuzzy* **tail between her**

---

★kumbaya 사람들 사이의 조화와 통합에 대해 노래하는 유명한 미국 포크 송의 제목. 또한, 이런 조화와 통합에 대해 낙관적으로 생각하는 사람들을 비꼬는 표현으로도 쓰인다.
✳whoopsie '아이고', '어머나'라는 뜻으로 놀람, 당황 등을 나타내는 소리.
✳fuzzy wuzzy '솜털 같은' 또는 '복슬복슬한'이라는 뜻.

legs to become— You're from Bunnyburrow? So let's say a carrot farmer? Sound about right?"

Judy stood **speechless**. She couldn't believe Nick had figured out her fears so quickly. A passing rhino almost pushed her down, **knock**ing her out of her thoughts.

"Be careful now," warned Nick. "Or it won't just be your dreams getting **crush**ed."

"Hey, hey!" she said, trying to **pull** herself **together**. "No one tells me what I can or can't be! Especially not some **jerk** who never had the **guts** to try and be anything more than a pawpsicle **hustler**."

"All right, look, everyone comes to Zootopia thinking they can be anything they want. Well, you can't. You can only be what you are." He pointed to himself. "**Sly** fox." Then he pointed to her. "**Dumb** bunny."

"I am *not* a dumb bunny."

"Right. And that's not wet cement.★"

Judy looked down to see that she was **ankle**-deep in **gooey** wet cement. She **sigh**ed in **dismay**.

---

★ cement 시멘트. 토목용이나 건축용으로 사용되는 무기질의 결합경화제를 말한다.

"You'll never be a real cop," Nick said **obnoxious**ly. "You're a cute meter maid, though. Maybe a **supervisor** one day. **Hang in there**."

**Frustrate**d, Judy watched as Nick walked off. Then she **set about** pulling her paws out of the cement.

**8**

*Shhhk! Shhhk!* Judy **dragg**ed her cement-covered paws across the welcome mat* outside her apartment before going in. A sad song filled the air when she turned on the radio. She **switch**ed **station**s. It was another sad song. And that was how her day was going. After listening to a few **depressing** songs, she dragged her feet over to the kitchen and **pop**ped in a Carrots for One **microwave** dinner.

*Beep! Beep!* Once it was done, she **peel**ed open the cover, **reveal**ing a single **shrivel**ed carrot. With her ears **droop**ing, Judy sat down at her small table and ate her dinner alone.

---

★welcome mat 현관 앞에 놓아 신발 바닥을 닦는 도어매트. 주로 'welcome'이라는 단어가 새겨져 있다.

*Brrring! Brrring!* Judy's cell phone rang. It was her parents calling for a video **chat**. She shook her head, **sigh**ed, and **forced** a smile before answering. "Oh, hey! It's my parents…," she said, trying to sound **upbeat**.

"There she is!" said Bonnie. "Hi, **sweetheart!**"

Stu's face popped onto the screen. "Hey there, Jude the Dude! How was your first day on the force?"

"It was real great," said Judy, knowing this was a complete lie.

"Yeah? Everything you ever hoped?" asked Bonnie.

"Absolutely, and more! Everyone's so nice. And I feel like I'm really making a difference—"

"Wait a second," said Stu, popping his head onto the screen again. "Holy cripes, Bonnie! Look at that!"

Bonnie **peer**ed into the screen trying to see what Stu was so excited about. "Oh my sweet heaven! Judy, are you a meter maid?"

Judy had forgotten she was still wearing her vest and that her hat was on the chair. She tried to **backpedal**. "What? Oh, this? No. It's just a **temporary**—"

"It's the safest job on the force!" **exclaim**ed Bonnie

happily.

"She's not a real cop! Our **prayers** have been answered!" said Stu, **overjoyed**.

"**Glorious** day!"

"Meter maid! Meter maid! Meter maid!" **chant**ed Stu.

"Dad. Dad!" said Judy, feeling uncomfortable and just wanting to end the conversation. "You know what? This has been great, guys, but it's been a long day—"

"That's right. You get some rest!" said Bonnie.

"Absolutely. Those meters aren't gonna maid themselves," added Stu.

They said goodnight and Judy **hung up**, feeling even sadder than she had before. As she took off her vest, she turned on more sad music. Through the wall, Oryx yelled: "Hey, bunny! Turn down that depressing music!"

"Leave the meter maid alone!" yelled Kudu. "Didn't you hear her conversation? She feels like a failure!"

Judy turned down the music as Oryx and Kudu continued to yell and **bicker**.

"Tomorrow's another day," she said quietly to herself.

"Yeah, but it might be worse!" yelled Oryx.

Exhausted, Judy **settle**d in for the night, wondering what tomorrow would bring.

The next day, Judy was back to ticketing cars parked at **expired** meters. She **plunk**ed a ticket down, and a moose yelled at her: "I was thirty seconds over!"

As another meter **ding**ed, Judy **scribble**d the ticket and placed it on a **tiny windshield**.

"You're a real hero, lady!" yelled an angry mouse.

*Ding!* Judy wrote out a third ticket, which a hippo picked up. Her small child looked at Judy and said, "My mommy says she wishes you were dead."

An angry driver shouted, "Uncool, rabbit. My **tax** dollars pay your **salary**."

Later, Judy got into her cart and turned the key. But

the engine wouldn't start. She **bang**ed her head against the **steer**ing **wheel**, making the horn **honk**.

"I am a real cop," she **mutter**ed weakly. "I am a real cop. I am a real cop. . . ."

"Hey hey!" called a **frantic** pig, running toward her. The pig **pound**ed on her cart window. "You! Bunny!"

"Sir, if you have a **grievance**, you may **contest** your **citation** in—" she responded **mechanical**ly.

"What're you talking about?" shouted the pig. "My shop! It just got **rob**bed! Look, he's **get**ting **away**! Well! Are you a cop or not?"

"Oh, yes," said Judy, **snap**ping **out of** it. "Don't worry, sir. I got this!"

She spotted a weasel running down the street, carrying a bag of stolen goods and jumped out of her cart.

"Stop!" she yelled, **chasing** the thief. "Stop in the name of the law!"

"Catch me if you can, cottontail!" shouted the weasel.

McHorn **screech**ed up in his **patrol** car. "This is **Officer** McHorn. We've got a 10-31,*" the rhinoceros said into his radio.

Judy **slid** right across McHorn's **hood** as she **rip**ped off her vest and hat and shouted, "I got **dibs!** Officer Hopps. I am in **pursuit!**"

She chased the weasel through Savanna<sup>✳</sup> Central, **dodging** giant elephants along the way.

Then the weasel **duck**ed into the tiny community of Little Rodentia. The large cops, who had joined in the chase, couldn't fit through the gate, but Judy was small enough to follow the weasel in.

"You!" she yelled **forcefully.** "Freeze!"

"Hey, meter maid! Wait for the real cops!" called McHorn.

Little Rodentia was packed with tiny **rodent**s, and Judy and the weasel looked like giants pounding down its small streets.

A mouse school bus **swerved** to avoid the weasel and flew skyward. Judy caught it in **midair, prevent**ing a **disaster.** The mice inside cheered as she gently placed the

---

★ 10-31 미국 경찰이 사용하는 부호체계인 ten code로, 10과 다른 숫자를 조합하여 무선 통신으로 현재 상황을 알릴 때 사용한다. 10−31은 용의자 추적 상황을 알리는 코드이다.
✳ savanna 우기와 건기가 뚜렷하게 구별되는 열대와 아열대 지방의 대초원.

bus on the ground. Judy watched the weasel jump off the top of a mouse building, **tip**ping it over. She **struggle**d to protect each and every building the weasel knocked into. Then he **leap**t on top of a moving mouse train!

"Bon voyage,* flatfoot!*" said the weasel with a **chuckle**, riding the train away.

But Judy wasn't about to **give up**. She ran even faster, until she was able to push him off the train. Rodents screamed and ran as Judy and the weasel came **barrel**ing through their **midst**.

"Hey!" she yelled. "Stop right there!"

"Have a donut, copper!*" the weasel said with a laugh as he **yank**ed a huge donut **sign** from the front of a shop. He **flung** it at Judy, but it missed and **bounce**d toward some shrews* coming out of Mousy's department store.

"Ohmygawd, did you see those leopard-print jeggings?*"

---

✦bon voyage 여행을 떠나는 사람에게 하는 인사말. 프랑스어로 '좋은 여행이 되세요!'라는 뜻이다.

✦flatfoot '경찰관'이라는 뜻의 속어.

✶copper '경찰관'이라는 뜻의 속어.

✦shrew 땃쥐. 생김새가 쥐를 닮았지만, 설치류는 아니며 두더지와 더 가까운 관계이다. 이빨이 날카로운 대못 모양인 것이 특징이다.

✦jeggings 청바지(jean)와 레깅스(leggings)의 합성어로, 다리에 딱 붙고 잘 늘어나는 특징을 가진 청바지를 의미한다.

said a **fashionable** shrew to her friends. She turned to see the donut bouncing toward her and screamed in **terror.** *"Aaaaaaaaaaagh!"*

A second before it **crush**ed the shrew, Judy moved in front of the donut and caught it in her arms. Then she turned to the shrew and said, "I love your hair."

"Awww . . . thank you," said the shrew **gratefull**y.

**Out of the corner of her eye**, Judy noticed that the weasel was about to get away. She threw the giant donut over his head and around his body, **trapping** him inside. The weasel was stuck!

It wasn't long before the weasel, still inside the donut, rolled through the front door of the ZPD lobby and hit Clawhauser's desk.

"I **pop**ped the weasel!" Judy exclaimed.

**Chief** Bogo yelled from the other room: "HOPPS!"

Like a kid in the **principal**'s office, Judy sat on a giant chair in front of Chief Bogo as he reviewed the report in front of him.

"**Abandon**ing your **post, inciting** a **scurry, reckless endanger**ment of rodents . . . but to be fair, you did stop a master **criminal** from stealing two dozen . . . um, let's see . . . **moldy** onions." Bogo looked straight at the bag on his desk that Judy had **confiscate**d from the **crook** she had stopped—Duke Weaselton.

"Hate to disagree with you, sir, but those aren't onions," Judy replied. "Those are a crocus* **varietal** called *Midnicampum holicithias.* They're a class C **botanical**, sir. I grew up in a family where plant **husbandry** was kind of a *thing.*"

"Shut your tiny mouth, now," said Bogo.

"Sir, I got the bad guy. That's my job."

"Your job is putting tickets on parked cars."

Bogo's **intercom click**ed as Clawhauser's voice came through. "Chief, uh, Mrs. Otterton's here to see you again."

"Not now," answered Bogo.

"Okay, I just didn't know if you wanted to take it this time—" said Clawhauser.

"Not now!"

Judy said, "Sir, I don't want to be a meter maid. I want

---

★ crocus 크로커스. 이른 봄에 노랑, 자주, 흰색의 작은 튤립 같은 꽃이 피는 식물.

to be a—"

"Do you think the **mayor** asked what I wanted before he **assign**ed you to me?" Bogo **interrupt**ed her.

"But, sir—"

"Life isn't some cartoon musical where you sing a little song and your **insipid** dreams magically come true. So **let it go**."

Just then a female otter,* Mrs. Otterton, **barged** in with Clawhauser **trail**ing behind, **wheezing**.

"Chief Bogo, please, just five minutes of your time," **plead**ed Mrs. Otterton.

"I'm sorry, sir, I tried to stop her; she is super **slippery**. I gotta go sit down," said Clawhauser, **pant**ing.

"Ma'am, as I've told you, we are doing everything we can," said Bogo.

"My husband has been missing for ten days," said Mrs. Otterton. "His name is Emmitt Otterton." She held up a family photo.

"Yes, I know," said Bogo.

---

★ otter 수달. 납작하고 둥근 머리, 둥근 코와 작은 귓바퀴를 지녔으며 짧은 네 발에 물갈퀴가 있어 헤엄을 잘 친다.

"He's a **florist**," she added. "We have two beautiful children. He would never just disappear."

"Ma'am, our **detective**s are very busy."

"Please. There's got to be somebody to find my Emmitt."

Bogo tried to calm Mrs. Otterton down, but nothing worked. She kept going on about her **concern** over Mr. Otterton's **disappearance**.

"I will find him," said Judy.

Bogo looked at Judy as if he was about to **explode**. He watched as Mrs. Otterton hugged Judy tightly.

"**Bless you**, bless you, little bunny!" she said, **relieved**. "You find my Emmitt and bring him home to me and my babies, please."

Bogo **grunt**ed and **usher**ed Mrs. Otterton back outside. "Mrs. Otterton? Please wait out here."

Bogo closed the door and turned to Judy, **furious**. "You're **fired**."

"What? Why?" she asked.

"**Insubordination**. Now, I'm going to open this door, and you are going to tell that otter you're a former meter maid with **delusion**s of **grandeur** who will not be taking the case."

Bogo opened the door and there was **Assistant** Mayor Bellwether, hugging Mrs. Otterton.

"I just heard Officer Hopps is taking the case!" said Bellwether happily. Bellwether pulled out her phone and began texting. "The **Mammal Inclusion Initiative** is really **pay**ing **off**! Mayor Lionheart is just going to be so **jazzed**!"

"Let's not tell the mayor just yet—" said Bogo.

"And I sent it, and it's done, so I did do that," interrupted Bellwether. "Well, I'd say the case is in good hands!" Bellwether smiled at Judy. "Us little guys really need to **stick together**! Right?"

"Like glue!" Judy responded.

"Good one," Bellwether said. "Just call me if you ever need anything. You've always got a friend at city hall, Judy. All right, bye bye!"

"Thank you, ma'am," Judy said.

Bogo **force**d a smile and closed the door. He turned to Judy, even angrier than before. "I will give you forty-eight hours," he said.

"YES!" cried Judy.

"That's two days to find Emmitt Otterton."

"Okay."

"But you **strike out**, you **resign**."

Judy couldn't believe what he was suggesting. "Oh, uh . . . ," She thought for a moment and then **nod**ded. "Okay . . . deal," she said.

"**Splendid**. Clawhauser will give you the complete case file," Bogo said.

Excited, Judy **rush**ed out to the front desk to **retrieve** the case file. "Here you go!" sang Clawhauser, handing her the file. "One missing otter!"

Judy opened the **folder** and her **jaw** dropped. Inside was a single piece of paper. "That's it?" she said in **disbelief**.

"Yikes!★ That is the smallest case file I've ever seen! **Lead**s: none. **Witness**es: none. And you're not in the computer system yet, so **resource**s: none." Clawhauser chuckled. "I hope you didn't **stake** your career on **crack**ing this one," he said, smiling.

Judy didn't smile back. Clawhauser took a **bite** of his

---

★yikes '이크', '어이구'라는 의미로 갑자기 놀라거나 겁을 먹었을 때 내는 소리.

donut and **crumbs land**ed on the picture inside the file.

"Last known **sighting** . . . ," she said, looking at the photo under Clawhauser's donut crumbs. The picture was from a **traffic** camera and showed Mr. Otterton on the street. Judy blew the crumbs off and noticed something about the picture. She **squint**ed. Still unable to see, she looked around. "Let me borrow that." She **grab**bed Clawhauser's empty soda bottle. She looked through it, using the glass at the bottom to **magnify** the image. Now she could see Mr. Otterton holding a frozen treat. She examined it and said **thoughtful**ly, "Pawpsicle."

"The **murder weapon!**" Clawhauser said, nodding.

"Get your pawpsicle . . . ," Judy said, thinking back to the **incident** with Nick.

"Yeah, because . . . What does that mean?" asked Clawhauser.

"It means I . . . have a *lead*." She headed out, leaving Clawhauser sitting at his desk, confused.

Judy drove around in her traffic cart until she found Nick pushing a baby **stroller** down the street. She smiled when she saw him. "Hi! Hello? It's me again!"

"Hey, it's Officer Toot-Toot," said Nick with a **smirk**.

"Ha-ha-ho!" Judy gave a **fake** laugh, **humor**ing him. "No, actually, it's Officer Hopps, and I'm here to ask you some questions about a case."

"What happened, meter maid?" asked Nick. "Did someone steal a traffic cone?* It wasn't me."

Nick walked on, pushing the stroller around the corner.

---

★traffic cone 도로의 공사 구간 등에 설치해 위험을 경고하는 원뿔 모양의 교통 표지물.

Judy pulled in front of him.

"Carrots, you're gonna wake the baby. I've got to get to work," said Nick.

"This is important, sir. I think your ten dollars' worth of pawpsicles can wait."

Nick faced her and raised his **eyebrow**s. "I make two hundred **bucks** a day, **Fluff**. Three hundred sixty-five days a year, since I was twelve. And time is money, so **hop** along."

"Please, just look at the picture," said Judy, holding up the picture of Mr. Otterton. "You sold Mr. Otterton that pawpsicle, right? Do you know him?"

"Lady, I know everybody. I also know that somewhere there's a toy store missing its **stuff**ed animals,★ so why don't you get back to your box?"

Judy's ears **droop**ed. "Fine," she said. "Then we'll have to do this the hard way." She **slap**ped a parking boot✱ onto the **wheel** of the stroller, **lock**ing it in place.

"Did you just boot my stroller?"

"Nicholas Wilde, you are under **arrest**," Judy said.

---

★ stuffed animal 솜으로 속을 채운 동물 모양의 봉제 인형.
✱ parking boot 주차 위반 차량의 바퀴에 끼워 움직이지 못하게 하는 바퀴 고정구.

Nick smiled, **amused**. "For what?

"**Felony tax evasion**," she replied.

Nick's smile quickly dropped.

"Yeah . . . ," continued Judy. "Two hundred dollars a day . . . three hundred sixty-five days a year . . . since you were twelve. That's two **decade**s, so times twenty . . . which is one million, four hundred sixty thousand—I think, I mean I am just a dumb bunny—but we are good at **multiply**ing. Anyway, according to your tax forms"—Judy presented some tax forms to Nick—"you reported, let me see here, zero. **Unfortunately**, lying on a **federal** form is a **punishable offense**. Five years **jail** time."

"Well, it's my word against yours," said Nick.

Judy held up a carrot-shaped pen and clicked a button. Suddenly, a **recording** of Nick's voice played from a speaker inside the pen: "I make two hundred bucks a day, Fluff. Three hundred sixty-five days a year, since I was twelve."

"Actually, it's your word against yours," Judy said. "And if you want this pen, you're going to **cooperate** with my **investigation** or the only place you'll be selling pawpsicles is the **prison cafeteria**." She **grin**ned. "It's called a **hustle**, sweetheart."

From the baby stroller, Finnick laughed **hysterically**. "She hustled you. She hustled you good. You're a cop now, Nick; you're gonna need one of these!" Finnick slapped his ZPD **badge** sticker on Nick. "Have fun working with the fuzz!*" Finnick jumped out of his stroller and walked away.

Nick took the photo of Mr. Otterton and looked at it.

"Start talking," said Judy.

"I don't know where he is. I only saw where he went."

Judy smiled broadly at him and **pat**ted the **passenger** seat of her cart. "Great, let's go."

"It's not **exact**ly a place for a cute little bunny," said Nick.

"Don't call me cute," Judy said. "Get in the car."

"Okay. You're the boss." Nick climbed in, and they headed off.

---

★fuzz '경찰'의 속어적 표현.

Nick led Judy to a place called the **Mystic Spring Oasis**. The **scent** of **incense waft**ed through the air inside the gates, and a yak* named Yax sat in **meditation**. Flies **buzz**ed around his unshowered body. "Oooooooohmmmmm," he **chant**ed. The **tone** of the buzzing flies seemed to **match** the tone of his voice. "Oooooooohmmmmm."

Judy approached Yax. "Hello! My name is—"

"Oh, you know, I'm gonna hit the **pause** button right there. We are all good on Bunny Scout Cookies,*" said

---

★ yak 야크. 중앙아시아에 사는 솟과의 동물로 다리가 짧고 온몸이 긴 털로 덮여 있는 것이 특징이다.

✻ Bunny Scout Cookies 걸스카우트 프로그램의 재정 확보를 위해 걸스카우트 대원들이 집집마다 돌아다니면서 판매하는 Girl Scout Cookies에서 Girl을 Bunny(토끼)로 바꾼 표현이다.

Yax, who talked slowly, almost as if he wasn't quite there.

"I am Officer Hopps, ZPD. I am looking for a missing mammal, Emmitt Otterton"—she showed him the picture—"who may have **frequent**ed this **establishment**."

Yax looked at the photo and his eyes **widen**ed, as if he was about to say something important.

"AH-CHOO!" he **sneeze**d, and flies **scatter**ed everywhere before returning to their place, **hover**ing around him. "Yep, Ol' Emmitt. Haven't seen him in a couple weeks. But hey, you should talk to his yoga **instructor**. I'd be happy to take you back." Yax nodded toward a different area of the club.

"Thank you so much," said Judy. "That would be a big—" Yax came around from behind the **counter**, and Judy was unable to complete her sentence when she saw what he was—or wasn't—wearing. "You are **naked**!"

"Huh? Oh, for sure, we're a Naturalist Club," said Yax **nonchalant**ly.

"Yeah, in Zootopia anyone can be anything . . . ," said Nick, **grin**ning, "and these guys, they be naked."

"Nanga's on the other side of the **pleasure** pool," offered

Yax. "Right this way, **folks**."

Judy's **jaw** dropped as she wondered what a pleasure pool was. When they got there, naked animals were sunning themselves, playing, and **lounging** around. Judy's eyes nearly popped out of her head at the **sight**. Nick **lean**ed over to her. "Does this make you uncomfortable? Because there is no **shame** in **calling it quits**. We could end our deal right now."

"Yes, there is," she said. She was **determine**d more than ever to stay on the case.

"Boy,* that's the **spirit**," **joke**d Nick.

Out in the **courtyard**, Judy tried to act normal. Her eyes **dart**ed around, looking for a **neutral** place to land.

"Yeah, some mammals say the naturalist life is **weird**," said Yax. "But you know what I say is weird? Clothes on animals! Here we go. As you can see, Nanga's an elephant, so she'll totally remember everything."

Nanga looked **curious**ly at the **newcomers**.

"Hey, Nanga, these **dude**s have some questions about

---

★ boy 소년, 남자아이를 나타내는 명사가 아니라, 놀람이나 기쁨을 나타내는 감탄사로 '어머나', '맙소사'라는 의미이다.

Emmitt the otter," said Yax.

"Who?" Nanga asked.

"Emmitt Otterton," Yax **prompt**ed. "Been coming to your yoga class for like six years."

"I have no memory of this beaver,*" Nanga **stated**.

"Yeah, he's an otter, actually," Judy corrected, looking over at Nick in **dismay**.

"He was here a couple Wednesdays ago. 'Member?" Yax prompted Nanga.

But the elephant just shook her head. "Nope."

"Yeah," Yax continued. "He was wearing a green cable-knit* sweater-**vest** and a new pair of corduroy* slacks.* Oh, and a paisley* tie, sweet Windsor knot,* real tight. Remember that, Nanga?"

Judy couldn't believe her luck. Yax was a **gold mine**! She **scramble**d to write everything down.

---

★ beaver 비버. 수중생활에 적응되어 있고 댐을 만드는 동물로 유명하다.
✻ cable-knit 새끼줄 모양의 니트.
✻ corduroy 흔히 코르덴이라 불리는 골이 지게 짠 옷감.
✻ slacks 정장용이 아닌 느슨하고 편하게 입을 수 있는 바지.
✻ paisley 직물 도안에 쓰이는, 세밀하고 다채로운 색상의 소용돌이 무늬를 말한다.
★ Windsor knot 윈저 노트. 넥타이 매듭 중에서 매듭 부위가 가장 크게 완성되는 것으로, 매듭 부분이 좌우 대칭으로 폭이 넓다.

"No," Nanga said again.

"Uh, ah, you didn't happen to catch the **license plate** number did you?" Judy asked.

"Oh, for sure," Yax nodded. "It was 29THD03."

Judy's pen moved quickly. "—03. Wow. This is a lot of great info.★ Thank you."

Yax smiled. "Told ya Nanga had a mind like a steel **trap**. I wish I had a memory like an elephant."

Outside the club, in Sahara **Square**, Nick smiled **smug**ly. "Well, I **had a ball**. You are welcome for the **clue**. And **seeing as how** any **moron** can run a plate,✸ I'll take that pen and **bid** you **adieu**."

Judy held out the pen, but as Nick went to reach for it, she realized something. She pulled it back before he could **swipe** it. "The plate . . . I can't run the plate. . . . I'm not in the system yet." She put the pen back in her pocket and smiled at Nick.

"Gimme the pen, please," said Nick.

---

★ info 'information(정보)'의 약어.
✸ run a plate 차량 번호판(a license plate)을 조회해서 소유주의 정보와 주소를 확인하는 일. 보통 경찰 사이에서 사용하는 은어이다.

"What was it you said? 'Any moron can run a plate'? **Gosh** . . . if only there were a moron around who **was up to** the task . . . ," she said.

"Rabbit, I did what you asked; you can't keep me **on the hook** forever," said Nick.

"No, not forever. I have"—Judy paused as she checked her phone—"thirty-six hours left to solve this case. Can you run the plate or not?"

Nick **stare**d at Judy, and then slowly grinned. "I just remembered, I have a **pal** at the DMV."

Inside the Department of Mammal **Vehicle**s, there was a huge line of animals waiting to be helped.

"They're all sloths!*" Judy **exclaim**ed, **noticing** the employees. Nick smiled. "You said this was going to be quick!"

"What? Are you saying that because he's a sloth, he can't be fast?" Nick said **innocent**ly. "I thought in Zootopia anyone could be anything."

Nick led Judy over to his friend, Flash, who was sitting behind the **counter** at one of the windows. "Flash, Flash,

---

★ sloth 나무늘보. 동작이 매우 느리고 나무에 매달려 나뭇잎, 열매 등을 따 먹는다. 주로 밤에 활동하며 하루에 18시간을 잔다.

hundred-yard★ **dash!**" said Nick. "**Buddy**, it's nice to see ya."

Flash looked at Nick for a long **beat**. "Nice to . . . see you . . . too," he said slowly.

"Flash, I'd love you to meet my friend. Darling, I seem to have forgotten your name."

"Officer Judy Hopps," said Judy, showing her badge. "ZPD. How are you?"

Flash looked at her and didn't respond for a good ten seconds. "I am . . . doing . . . just—"

Judy couldn't take it. "Fine?" she offered, trying to move the conversation along.

". . . as well . . . as . . . I can . . . be. What—" Flash continued.

"**Hang in there**," said Nick, loving every second.

". . . can I . . . do . . ."

"Well, I was hoping you could run a **plate**—"

". . . for you . . ."

"Well, I was hoping you could—"

---

★ yard 거리의 단위인 야드. 1야드는 0.9144미터이다.

"... today?" Flash asked, finally completing his sentence.

"Well, I was hoping you could run a plate for us. We're in a really big hurry," answered Judy.

Flash waited a moment before beginning his response. "Sure. What's the . . . plate—"

"Two nine—" Judy began.

". . . number?" asked Flash.

Judy took a deep breath. "29THD03."

Flash took another moment before repeating it. "Two . . . nine . . ."

"THD03," said Judy.

"T," said Flash.

It took quite a while for Flash to enter the first part of the **license** plate number into the system. Just as he was about to **punch** in the last **digit**, Nick interrupted him. "Hey, Flash, you wanna hear a **joke**?"

"No!" Judy **yell**ed.

"What do you call a three-**hump**ed camel?★"

"I don't . . . know. What do . . . you call . . . a—"

---

★ camel 낙타. 목과 다리가 길며 등에 지방을 저장하는 혹이 있으며 오랜 시간 물 없이도 견딜 수 있다.

"Three-humped camel," said Judy quickly, trying to get the joke out of the way.

". . . three-humped . . . camel?" said Flash.

"**Pregnant**," answered Nick.

Flash showed no reaction at first, but then he slowly raised his head as a smile **crept** across his face. "Ha . . . ha . . . ha . . . ha . . ."

Judy's **impatience** grew. "Ha, ha, yes, very funny, very funny. Can we please just focus on the—"

Flash turned toward the sloth next to him. "Hey, Priscilla . . ."

"Yes . . . Flash?" answered Priscilla, just as slowly.

"What . . . do . . . you call . . . a—"

"A three-humped camel? Pregnant!" shouted Judy, thoroughly **frustrated**.

"Three . . . humped . . ."

Judy was **losing her mind**. "*Aaaaaaaaaagh!*"

Hours after they'd entered, a dot-matrix printer* slowly **spat** out the address for the license plate number.

"Here you . . . ," said Flash, handing it to Judy.

"Yeah, yeah, yeah . . . thank you!" she said.

". . . go."

"29THD03," said Judy, **frantic**ally reading the **printout**. "It's **register**ed to . . . Tundratown **Limo**-Service? A limo took Otterton, and the limo's in Tundratown— It's in Tundratown!"

"Way to hustle, buddy," Nick said to Flash. "I love you. I owe you."

"Hurry, we gotta beat the rush hour and—" Judy said as she hurried through the door to get outside. "IT'S NIGHT!" She looked at the sky in **awe**. It was completely dark.

They had been in there for hours! Judy was **run**ning **out of** time.

---

★ dot-matrix printer 도트 매트릭스 프린터. 잉크 리본에 충격을 가하는 방법으로 글자를 인쇄하는 프린터. 소음이 심하며 출력속도가 비교적 느리다.

**J**udy and Nick drove to **frigid** Tundratown, where everything was covered in snow and ice. When they found Tundratown **Limo**-Service, it was **lock**ed up tight.

"Closed," Judy said, **gesturing** to the lock on the gate. "Great."

"And I will **bet** you don't have a **warrant** to get in. Hmm? Darn it. It's a **bummer**," said Nick.

"You **wasted** the day **on purpose**," said Judy.

"Madam, I have a **fake** badge. I would never **impede** your pretend **investigation**."

"It is not a pretend investigation!" Judy said, showing Nick the picture of Otterton. "Look! See! See him? This otter is missing!"

"Well, then they should have gotten a real **cop** to find him."

She wasn't going to let Nick **get to** her. "What is your problem?" she asked. "Does seeing me fail somehow make you feel better about your own sad, **miserable** life?"

Nick appeared to consider her question before answering. "It does. One hundred percent. Now . . . since you're **sans** warrant, I guess we're done?"

Judy **sigh**ed, **defeat**ed. "Fine," she said. "We are done. Here's your pen." She threw the pen over the fence, into the lot.

"Hey," said Nick, staring at her, **puzzled**. "First off, you throw like a bunny, and second, you are a very **sore loser**." Nick started to climb over the fence. "See you later, **Officer Fluff**. So sad this is over. Wish I could've helped more—"

Nick jumped down to the other side of the fence and reached for the pen, but Judy was already there, **beat**ing him to it.

"The thing is, " Judy said, "you don't need a warrant if you have **probable** cause. And I'm pretty sure I saw a **shifty**

**lowlife** climbing the fence, so you're helping plenty. Come on," she said, heading off as she **whistled** a **merry tune.**

Nick watched her, **annoyed,** but his face also showed a **morsel** of **respect** for her **trick.**

In the **parking lot,** Nick **wiped** snow off the back of a bumper* to show the **plate.**

"29THD03," read Judy. "This is it."

The **limousine** was actually a "refrigousine." It had a heavy **refrigerator** door and was cold inside. Judy pulled out an **evidence** bag with **tweezers** as she and Nick **snoop**ed around the **chilly** limo.

"Polar bear* **fur,**" she said, holding up a piece of fur trapped in her tweezers.

"OH MY GOD!" said Nick.

"What? What!" exclaimed Judy, **whirl**ing to see the source of Nick's excitement. He had opened the glove

---

★ bumper 범퍼. 차 앞뒤에 장착되어 차체를 보호하기 위해서 마련된 장치로, 충돌했을 때 순간 충격을 흡수하는 작용을 한다.
✳ polar bear 북극곰. 북극권에 분포하며 섬 또는 대륙의 해안이나 툰드라에 서식한다.

compartment.

"*The **Velvety Pipes** of Jerry Vole!*★" said Nick, showing her CDs. "But on CD? Who still uses CDs?"

Judy **roll**ed **her eyes** and went back to collecting real **clue**s. Nick lowered the back **partition**, and his **eyebrow**s shot up. "Carrots, if your otter was here . . . he had a very bad day."

Nick and Judy stared at the **backseat**. It had been **shred**ded! Violent-looking **claw mark**s were **scraped** across it.

"You ever seen anything like this?" asked Judy.

Nick shook his head, actually **concern**ed. "No."

Judy **spot**ted a wallet on the floor and picked it up. She opened it to find Mr. Otterton's driver's **license** and business cards for his **floral** shop. "This is him! Emmitt Otterton. He was definitely here. What do you think happened?"

Nick shook his head, **stump**ed. Then his eyes **drift**ed to the cocktail glasses at the bar inside the limo. They were **etch**ed with the letter *B*.

---

★ vole 들쥐. 다른 쥐에 비해 비교적 귀와 꼬리가 짧고 초원 등에 서식하는 것이 특징이다.

"Wait a minute," said Nick **suspiciou**sly. "Polar bear fur . . . Rat Pack music . . . **fancy** cups . . ." He turned to Judy. "I know whose car this is. We gotta go."

"Why? Whose car is it?" she asked.

Nick **rush**ed around the limo, nervously trying to put everything back the way they found it. "The most dangerous crime boss in Tundratown. They call him Mr. Big, and *he* does *not* like me, so we've gotta go!"

"I'm not leaving," said Judy. "This is a crime **scene**."

"Well, it's gonna be an even bigger crime scene if Mr. Big finds me, so we are leaving right now!"

Nick **made a break** for the limo door, but when he opened it, two big polar bears looked down at him. "Raymond! And is that Kevin?" said Nick, trying to sound excited. "Long time no see! And speaking of no see, how about you forget you saw me? For old times' **sake**?"

Without saying a word, the polar bears **yank**ed Nick and Judy out of the limo. They **shove**d them into a car and **sandwich**ed Nick and Judy between them.

"What did you do to make Mr. Big so mad at you?" Judy asked Nick.

"I, uh, may or may not have sold him a very expensive wool* rug . . .* that was made from the fur of a . . . skunk's* **butt**," Nick said quietly.

"Sweet cheese and crackers,*" said Judy.

A short time later, the car pulled through a **guard**ed **security** gate into a giant **residential compound** that was the home of Mr. Big.

---

★ wool 양모(羊毛). 곱슬거리고 보온성과 흡습성이 강하며, 모사나 모직물의 원료가 된다.
✳ rug 러그. 바닥에 까는 직물.
✸ skunk 스컹크. 족제빗과의 동물로 몸이 땅딸막하며 꼬리가 길고 귀가 작다. 위험에 처하면 항문선에서 악취가 강한 황금색 액체를 발사한다.
✳ sweet cheese and crackers '세상에', '이럴 수가'라는 뜻의 'sweet Jesus Christ'의 다른 표현으로 놀라움이나 실망, 불신 등을 나타낸다.

**14**

Judy and Nick were led inside the house and into a **lavish**ly decorated office. A large polar bear entered the room.

"Is that Mr. Big?" Judy **whisper**ed to Nick.

"No," he answered.

An even bigger polar bear **lumber**ed in behind. "What about him? Is that him?" Judy asked.

"No," said Nick, **frustrate**d.

An even bigger polar bear showed up, following the others. "Okay, that's gotta be him," Judy said.

"Stop talking, stop talking, stop talking—"

The largest polar bear held a **teeny tiny** chair in his giant **paw**. Sitting on the chair was a little **Arctic** shrew.*

ZOOTOPIA

"Mr. Big, sir, this is a simple misunder—" Nick started.

Judy stared at the tiny shrew in wide-eyed surprise. *He was Mr. Big?*

Mr. Big held out his tiny finger, and Nick kissed the ring **wrap**ped around it.

"This is a simple **misunderstanding**," said Nick.

Mr. Big **motion**ed for Nick to be quiet. "You come here un**announced** . . . on the day my daughter is to be married?" Mr. Big's **raspy** voice had an **authoritative tone** to it, but it also sounded like his body: very tiny.

"Well, actually, we were brought here against our will, so. . . . Point is, I did not know it was your car, and I certainly did not know about your daughter's wedding," Nick said, **chuckling** nervously.

"I trusted you, Nicky. I welcomed you into my home. We **broke bread** together. Gram-mama made you her cannoli.*" Mr. Big **frown**ed and **scratch**ed his **chin** as he looked at Nick with cold eyes. "And how did you **repay** my

---

★Arctic shrew 북극뒤쥐. 밤에 가장 활동적이고 땅 위에서 혼자 생활하며 식욕이 왕성한 것이 특징이다.

✳cannoli 카놀리. 귤, 초콜릿, 땅콩, 달콤한 치즈 등으로 속을 만들어 파이 껍질로 싼 다음 튀긴 후식.

generosity? With a rug . . . made from the **butt** of a skunk. A skunk-butt rug. You **disrespect**ed me. You disrespected my gram-mama, who I **buried** in that skunk-butt rug. I told you never to show your face here again, but here you are, **snoop**ing around with this . . ." Mr. Big gestured to Judy. "What are you, a performer? What's with the **costume?**"

Judy tried to answer. "Sir, I am a co—"

"Mime!★" Nick shouted, **cut**ting her **off.** "She is a mime. This mime cannot speak. You can't speak if you're a mime."

"No," said Judy. "I am a cop."

Mr. Big **shift**ed in his tiny chair, **agitated.**

"And I'm on the Emmitt Otterton case. My **evidence** puts him in your car, so **intimidate** me all you want; I'm going to find out what you did to that otter if it's the last thing I do."

Mr. Big considered Judy and **grunt**ed. "Then I have only one request: say hello to Gram-mama. Ice 'em!" he shouted to the polar bears.

"Whoa! I didn't see nothing! I'm not saying nothing!"

---

★ mime 무언극. 언어를 사용하지 않고 몸짓과 표정만으로 표현하는 연기를 가리킨다. 무언극을 하는 배우를 말할 때 사용하기도 한다.

Nick said, trying to **squirm** his way **out of** death by ice.

"And you never will," said Mr. Big coolly.

The polar bears picked Judy and Nick up, ready to throw them down into a **freezing pit** of ice and water the bears had opened in front of Mr. Big's desk.

"Please!" Nick **begg**ed. "No, no, no! If you're mad at me about the rug, I've got more rugs!"

The polar bears held Nick and Judy over the pit. Then Mr. Big's daughter, Fru Fru, who was as tiny as her father, entered, wearing a wedding **gown**.

"Oh, Daddy, it's time for our dance," she said. She noticed Judy and Nick and sighed, clearly annoyed. "What did we say? No icing anyone at my wedding."

"I have to, baby," said Mr. Big. "Daddy has to." Then he turned to Nick and Judy and calmly said, "Ice 'em."

Nick and Judy screamed.

"Wait. WAIT!" Fru Fru shouted. "I know her. She's the bunny who saved my life yesterday. From that giant donut."

It was the stylish shrew from Little Rodentia.

"This bunny?" asked Mr. Big.

"Yes!" She turned to Judy. "Hi," she said sweetly.

"Hi," said Judy. "I love your dress."

"Aw, thank you," said Fru Fru.

Mr. Big motioned to the polar bears. "Put 'em down." Then he turned to Judy. "You have done me a great service. I will help you find the otter. I will take your kindness . . . and **pay it forward**."

Nick stood there, **dumbfounded** . . . and extremely happy not to be in a pit of ice.

**A**rctic animals danced as Fru Fru and her **groom fed** each other cake. Nick and Judy looked like giants as they sat at the **head table**, next to Mr. Big.

"Otterton is my **florist**," said Mr. Big. "He's like a part of the family. He had something important he wanted to discuss. That's why I sent that car to **pick** him **up**. But he never arrived."

"Because he was attacked," said Judy.

"No . . . *he* attacked," Mr. Big explained. "He went crazy. **Rip**ped up the car, **scare**d my driver half to death, and disappeared into the night."

"He's a sweet little otter," said Judy.

"My child, we may be **evolved** . . . but deep down, we are still animals."

Nick and Judy exchanged a worried look.

"You want to find Otterton . . . talk to the driver of the car. His name is Manchas, lives in the Rainforest **District**. Only he can tell you more."

Judy and Nick left the wedding and headed straight for the **lush, humid** Rainforest District in search of their next **clue**.

As the steam trees **pump**ed a **steady stream** of **mist** into the rainforest air, Judy and Nick climbed higher and higher. They followed a **wind**ing road to a home high up in the **canopy**. Once the **steamy fog** cleared, they could see Manchas's **moss**-covered apartment.

"Mr. Manchas?" Judy called, after ringing the doorbell. "Judy Hopps, ZPD. I'd like to ask you some questions about Emmitt Otterton." She **knock**ed on the door as Nick **snoop**ed through Manchas's mailbox.

"He's a kitty," said Nick, holding up an issue of *Cat*

*Fancy* magazine. "Hey, buddy, I got a can of tuna out here. Open the door, we'll **talk** it **out**—"

"Not every cat likes tuna," said Judy.

"Oh, right, got it," said Nick. He turned back to the door. "Buddy, I got a ball of **yarn** out here—"

Judy **playfully punch**ed Nick. "Sir, my partner's an **idiot**. You're not in trouble. We just want to know what happened to Emmitt Otterton."

Finally, the door slowly **creak**ed open, just a **crack**. "You should be asking . . . what happened to *me*," said a voice from inside.

The chain lock **prevent**ed the door from opening all the way. Through the space, they could see that Manchas was a big jaguar and he had been badly **beat**en, with **bruise**s, **scratch**es, and a **black eye**.

"Whoa. A **teensy** otter . . . did that?" asked Nick.

"What . . . happened?" Judy asked.

Manchas described the **scene**, sounding **haunted**. Like he was **reliving** it. "He was an *animal*, down on all fours. He was a **savage**. There was no warning, just kept yelling about the 'night **howl**ers, the night howlers,' over and over."

Nick and Judy shared a look. "Oh. Wow. That's crazy, because that is actually why we came to talk to you . . . about the night howlers. Right?" said Judy, pumping for more information.

"Yes," said Nick, picking up on Judy's cue. "Absolutely. Whole ride over here we're sitting there going, *night howler* this, *night howler* that. Tell him."

"Yup. So you just open the door and tell us what you know, and we will tell you what we know," Judy persuaded. "Okay?"

Manchas considered a moment and then shut the door.

As he unlocked each of the locks from inside, Nick glanced at Judy, impressed. "You're not as dumb as you look," he said.

With a smile, she punched him on the arm. Hard.

They heard Manchas make a strange grunting noise.

"Mr. Manchas?" said Judy. "Are you okay?"

A loud thud sounded. Then the door creaked and opened just an inch. Judy slowly pushed it and saw Manchas hunched over in the middle of the room.

"Buddy?" Nick asked.

With a low **growl**, Manchas turned to them. His eyes were huge. He was SAVAGE! He **raced** at Nick and Judy like a **primal predator**.

"Run. *RUN!*" Judy screamed.

**N**ick and Judy ran for their lives as Manchas **chase**d them.

"What is wrong with him?" shouted Nick.

"I don't know!"

They ran across a **slippery** suspension bridge★ with Manchas close behind. Nick stopped. "We're not gonna **make it!**"

"Jump!" Judy **yell**ed.

They **leapt** off the bridge and **land**ed on a low **branch**. Then they **duck**ed into a **hollow log**, trying to hide, but Manchas continued to **stalk** them. Judy **frantic**ally picked

---

★ suspension bridge 현수교. 상판의 양쪽 끝에 위치한 탑과 탑 사이에 설치된 케이블이 도로를 지지하는 다리.

up her police radio. "Officer Hopps to **dispatch**! Clawhauser, can you hear me?"

Inside the police **station**, Clawhauser was **casually** **chat**ting with a **coworker** as he showed him a video on his phone.

"Have you seen Gazelle's new video—are you familiar with Gazelle?" Clawhauser asked the coworker, not seeing the red light **blink**ing on his phone. "Greatest singer of our **lifetime**—angel with **horn**s. Yeah, you gotta **check** it **out**. So good. Do you see who's beside her right now?" He pointed to the screen, where he was dancing on a stage with Gazelle.

"Wow. You are one hot dancer," Gazelle's voice started, finishing with a **robotic**-type voice, "Benjamin Clawhauser."

"It's me!" Clawhauser **exclaim**ed. "Did you think it was real? It looks so real! It's not—it's just a new app." He **chuckl**ed. Then he finally **notice**d his phone and **click**ed the speaker button. "**Hold on**—"

"Clawhauser!" Judy's voice rang out. Manchas, trying to get inside the log, took a **swipe** at her. "We have a 10-91!* Jaguar gone savage! Vine and Tu-junga!"

"It's Tu-HUN-ga!" shouted Nick.

Manchas took another swipe at Judy, this time **rip**ping her radio out of her hands. Nick and Judy **scrambl**ed out of the log and continued to run.

"Sending **back up**! Hopps? HOPPS?!" said Clawhauser, hearing the **racket** on the other end.

Nick and Judy spotted a gondola* station. "There!" Judy yelled. "Head to the sky**tram**s!"

They ran toward the gondolas. Judy **dart**ed out of Manchas's way but **slip**ped and got separated from Nick.

"Get in! Carrots? Carrots!" Nick called, trying to hold on to the gondola. But it **pull**ed **away**.

"Go!" shouted Judy, **struggling** to **regain** her **footing** on the wet, slippery surface of the bridge.

Nick backed up and Manchas moved toward him, as if stalking his **prey**. "**Buddy**, one predator to another, if I **offend**ed you with the tuna thing, I meant no **disrespe**—"

Nick screamed as Manchas **charged** at him full speed.

---

★ 10-91 용의자나 조사대상자를 붙잡았다는 것을 알리는 코드.

✷ gondola 곤돌라. 스키장이나 산악지대에서 사용되는 리프트의 일종으로 케이블에 연결되어 움직이는 운송수단이다.

A **split second** before he reached Nick—*clank!* Manchas was yanked back by a **handcuff** on his back **paw**. Judy had **cuff**ed him to a metal **post**! Nick couldn't believe it—Judy had saved his life.

"I can tell you're **tense**, so I'm just gonna give you a little personal space," Nick said to Manchas.

Manchas struggled angrily, knocking Nick and Judy over the **edge** of the **walkway**. Judy **grab**bed on to a **vine** with one arm and struggled to hold Nick with her other. As the two **dangle**d over the **canopy**, Nick looked at the **bottomless abyss** below. Judy's mind **race**d as she tried to **figure out** what to do next.

"Rabbit, whatever you do, do not **let go**!" shouted Nick.

"I'm gonna let go!" said Judy.

"No . . . you what? You must have **misunderstood** me. I said don't—"

"One, two," Judy said, **count**ing **off** as she started them **swing**ing.

"RABBIT!"

She let go and swung them over to a **net** made of vines. It supported their weight for a moment. But then—*snap!*

The vines broke and they **plummet**ed toward the ground! Luckily, a **cluster** of vines had gotten **tangle**d around their legs and stopped them right before they hit the rainforest floor.

**Siren**s rang out as a **convoy** of police cars **screech**ed to a **halt**. Out of one stepped **Chief** Bogo. Judy smiled. The **cavalry** had arrived!

"Well, this should be good," said Bogo as he **stare**d at Judy and Nick, who hung upside down, **suspend**ed from vines, in front of him.

**J**udy **confident**ly led the **cops** up to the **canopy**. "I thought this was just a missing **mammal** case, but it's way bigger. Mr. Otterton did not just disappear. I believe he and this jaguar . . . they went savage, sir."

Bogo **scoff**ed. "Savage? This isn't the Stone Age,★ Hopps. Animals don't go savage."

"I thought so, too, until I saw this." Judy turned the corner where she had **handcuff**ed Manchas—but he was gone! Even the handcuffs had **vanish**ed.

"He was right here," she said, **confus**ed.

---

★Stone Age 석기시대. 돌을 이용하여 도구를 만들어 쓰던 시대를 말한다.

"The 'savage' jaguar," said Bogo, scoffing once again.

"Sir, I know what I saw. He almost killed us," said Judy.

"Or maybe an **aggressive** predator looks savage to you rabbits," Bogo said. He called out to the other **officers**, "Let's go."

"Wait—sir, I'm not the only one who saw him!"

Judy called to Nick, but before he could explain, Bogo said, "You think I'm going to believe a fox?"

"Well, he was a **key witness**, and I **enlist**ed his services," Judy said.

Bogo shook his head, **annoyed**. "Two days to find the otter . . . or you quit . . . that was the deal. **Badge**," he said, waiting for her to hand her badge over.

Nick watched Judy **stare** at Bogo's **outstretched** hand. "Sir, we . . ."

"*Badge*," said Bogo firmly.

Judy slowly reached for it as Nick spoke up. "Uh, no," he said.

Bogo **glare**d at Nick. "What did you say, fox?"

"Sorry, what I said was 'no.' She will not be giving you that badge," said Nick. "Look, you gave her a **clown vest** and a three-**wheel joke-mobile** and two days to solve a case you guys haven't **crack**ed in two weeks? Yeah, no wonder she needed to get help from a fox. None of you guys were gonna help her, were you?"

Judy stared at Nick. She couldn't believe he was **stick**ing **up for** her. Bogo stood silently.

"Here's the thing, Chief. You gave her forty-eight hours, so **technically** we still have ten left to find our Mr. Otterton . . . and that's **exact**ly what we are gonna do. So if you'll excuse us . . . we have a very big **lead** to follow and a case to crack. Good day."

Nick turned to Judy. "Officer Hopps?" He guided her to a passing gondola, leaving Bogo and the rest of the officers **stun**ned.

"Thank you," she said as the two sat in the gondola while it **soar**ed over the Rainforest District.

"Never let them see that they **get to** you," said Nick.

Surprised, Judy turned to Nick. "So things get to you?"

"No . . . I mean, not anymore," said Nick. "But I was small and **emotional**ly **unbalanced** like you once."

"Har-har," said Judy.

"No, it's true. I think I was eight, maybe nine, and all I wanted to do was join the Junior Ranger Scouts."

Nick decided to tell Judy a story about when he was a kid. "So my mom **scraped** together enough money to buy me a **brand-new uniform**." Nick explained how badly he wanted to **fit in**—even though he was the only predator in the **troop**. "I was gonna be part of a **pack**," he said.

Nick described the **scene**. He was taking the **oath** with the scouts when the other kids suddenly **tackle**d him, yelling, "Get him! Get that pred!* **Muzzle** him!"

They **strap**ped a muzzle onto his **snout** and continued to **mock** him. "If you thought we'd ever trust a fox without a muzzle, you're even dumber than you look," one of them had **taunt**ed.

When they finally **let** him **go**, he ran away, **limp**ing, with his uniform **torn** to pieces.

"I learned two things that day," said Nick, lost in the terrible memory. "One, I was never going to let anyone see that they got to me."

---

★ pred 'predator(포식자)'의 약어.

"And two?" Judy **prod**ded.

"If the world's only gonna see a fox as **shifty** and **untrustworthy**, there's no point trying to be anything else."

"Nick," said Judy gently. "You are so much more than that." She touched his arm as the gondola **pierce**d through the clouds. They **gaze**d down at the busy city **buzz**ing below.

"Boy, look at that **traffic** down there," said Nick, changing the subject. "How about we go to Chuck in Traffic Central," Nick continued, pretending to be a **cheesy** radio **announcer**. "Chuck, how are things looking on those **Jam Cam**s?"

"Nick, I'm glad you told me," said Judy.

"Wait! The Jam Cams!" said Nick **urgent**ly.

"Seriously, it's okay," said Judy.

"N-no, shh-**shush**! There are traffic cameras everywhere. All over the canopy. Whatever happened to that jaguar—"

"The traffic cameras would have caught it!" said Judy, excitedly, suddenly realizing what Nick meant.

"Bingo!★" said Nick.

---

★bingo '좋았어', '해냈어'라는 뜻으로, 찾던 물건을 찾거나 하려던 일을 해냈을 때 하는 말이다.

Judy chucked him on the arm, impressed. "Pretty sneaky, Slick."

"However. If you didn't have access to the system before, I doubt Chief Buffalo Butt is gonna give it to you now."

"No. But I've got a friend at city hall who might!" Judy smiled, feeling hopeful again.

It didn't take long for Judy and Nick to find **Assistant Mayor** Bellwether in city hall. She was **struggling** to hold a **stack** of files while **keep**ing **up** with Mayor Lionheart.

"Sir?" said Bellwether. "If we could just review these very important—"

As Bellwether continued to struggle and **dodge** out of the way inside the busy lobby, she almost stepped on a little mouse.

"Oh, I'm sorry . . . sir!"

"I heard you, Bellwether," said Lionheart **impatient**ly. "Just take care of it, okay?" He set a **folder** on top of her huge stack. "And clear my afternoon. I'm going out."

"But, sir, you have a meeting with **Herd**s and **Grazing**. . . .
Sir—"

Lionheart continued through the door, letting it **slam**
right in Bellwether's face. All the files she was carrying were
knocked to the floor.

"Oh, mutton chops,* " she said, trying to collect the
**scatter**ed pieces of paper.

"Assistant Mayor Bellwether," said Judy, approaching
her. "We need your help."

Bellwether led them to her **tiny, cramp**ed office. Judy
and Nick looked around, surprised. Bellwether's office was
actually a **janitor**'s **closet**!

"We just need to get into the **traffic** camera database,* "
Judy said as Bellwether typed on the keyboard of her
computer.

Nick **barely** touched the wool **puff** on top of Bellwether's
head and **whisper**ed, "Sooo **fluffy**!" He was **mesmeriz**ed.
"Sheep never let me this close—so fluffy—like cotton

---

★ mutton chop 원래는 양의 갈비살이라는 뜻이지만, 여기에서는 놀람이나 탄식을 나타내는 '이런',
'아이고'라는 의미로 사용되었다.
✻ database 데이터베이스. 상호 관련된 데이터를 정리, 통합하여 컴퓨터 처리가 가능한 형태로 만
든 파일 또는 그 집합체.

candy—*"

"You can't touch that! Stop it!" **scold**ed Judy, **swat**ting his hand away as she tried to keep Bellwether from seeing Nick.

"Where to?" Bellwether asked as she pulled up traffic cameras for the whole city. She looked up at Judy, catching the rabbit in mid-swat.

"Rainforest **District**. Vine and Tujunga."

Nick and Judy shared a smiled. This time, Judy had **pronounce**d *Tujunga* correctly.

"This is so exciting, actually. Well, you know, I never get to do anything this important," said Bellwether.

"You're the assistant mayor of Zootopia," said Judy.

"Oh, I'm more of a **glorified secretary**," said Bellwether. "I think Mayor Lionheart just wanted the sheep **vote**. . . . But he did get me that nice **mug**." She proudly pointed to a mug that read WORLD'S GREATEST ~~DAD~~ ASSISTANT MAYOR.

"Smellwether!" shouted Mayor Lionheart through the **intercom**.

---

★ cotton candy 솜사탕. 설탕을 불에 녹인 후 막대기에 감아 솜 모양으로 만든 사탕.

Bellwether **cringed** as she got up. "Oh, that's a fun little name he uses. I called him Lion**fart** once. He didn't care for that." She **press**ed the button on the intercom. "Yes, sir?"

"I thought you were going to cancel my afternoon!" Lionheart yelled.

"Oh, dear . . . I better go. Let me know what you find. It was really nice for me to—"

"While we're young, Smellwether!" the mayor's voice **boom**ed again as she opened the door and hurried out.

"Well, I'm gonna need a **lint** brush," said Nick.

"Oh **shush**," said Judy. "Okay. Traffic cameras. Tujunga, Tujunga . . . we're in."

Nick and Judy watched the **footage onscreen**. They saw Manchas acting wild, and then . . . a black **van pull**ed **up**, **skid**ding to a stop.

"Who are these guys?" Judy asked.

"Timber wolves.* Look at these dum-dums.*"

They watched as wolves got out of the van and **trapp**ed Manchas with a **net**! Judy **gasp**ed, but Nick just shook his

---

★timber wolf 팀버 늑대. 시각, 후각, 청각 등 여러 감각을 동원해 무리 간 의사소통을 한다.
✻dum-dum '얼간이', '바보'라는 뜻의 속어.

head.

"**Bet** you a nickel\* one of them's gonna **howl**," Nick said.

One of the wolves howled.

"There it is. What is with wolves and howling?" he asked.

"Howlers. Night howlers," said Judy. "That's what Manchas was afraid of—wolves! The wolves are the night howlers. If they took Manchas—"

"I bet they took Otterton, too," said Nick.

"All we've gotta do is find out where they went," said Judy, examining the footage. As the wolves drove off, they disappeared through a tunnel and didn't come out the other side. "Wait. Where'd they go?"

Nick **squint**ed at the picture. "You know, if I wanted to avoid **surveillance** because I was doing something **illegal**—which I never have—I'd use the **maintenance** tunnel 6B, which would put them out . . ." Nick clicked over to another camera's footage, then another, and another . . . and then

---

★nickel 미국이나 캐나다에서 쓰이는 5센트 동전.

the wolves **emerged** in the van! "Right there."

"Look at you," Judy said, impressed. "Junior **Detective**. You know, I think you'd actually make a pretty good cop."

"How **dare** you," Nick said in **mock horror**, trying not to smile.

Judy clicked through some more surveillance videos, **track**ing the wolves through **alleys** and back roads. "They're heading out of town," she said. "Where does that road go?"

"It's one of two places: it's either that very, very **scary** old building . . . or a Beaver Renaissance Faire.*"

---

★Renaissance Faire 르네상스 축제. 중세 르네상스 시대의 생활 및 문화를 재현하는 축제.

Nick and Judy found the **mysterious** road and followed it. They stopped and watched from a **distance** as a **van** drove past a gated **checkpoint**. Beyond the gate was a **creepy** old building called Cliffside **Asylum** that **perch**ed high on a **cliff** over the ocean.

"Why couldn't you be a Beaver Renaissance Faire?" Nick said quietly.

The two slowly **ventured** toward the asylum, **sneak**ing up to the **guard**ed gate. They could see two wolves **station**ed inside. Nick **motion**ed that he was going to try and **tiptoe** past. He **start**ed **off**, but as he got closer, one of the wolves **sniff**ed the air, **pick**ing **up on** his **scent**. Nick grabbed a piece of **driftwood** to use as a **weapon** as the wolf began searching for the source of the scent. But before the wolf could find Nick, a howl sounded in the distance, grabbing the wolf's attention. "Ooooooooo!"

It was Judy, hidden beneath the cliffs!

Hearing the sound, the wolf couldn't help but howl back.

Another guard approached and said sharply, "Quit it, Gary. You're gonna start a howl."

"I didn't start it. Ooooooooo!" said Gary.

Unable to control it, the other guard howled back. Soon more and more wolves joined in, howling away.

Judy whispered to Nick, "Come on!" They used the **distraction** to jump the fence and sneak by the guards.

"Clever bunny," said Nick, **impress**ed.

As they **scrambled** over the **slippery** rocks, Nick nearly **slid** down a **waterfall**. They searched for a way into the building and **spot**ted a large **pipe**. Climbing inside, they walked until they **emerged** in the asylum. The dark **cavernous** room was full of old, **rusty medical equipment**.

"Looks like this was a hospital," said Judy.

She shined her light down a **corridor** and saw a metal door at the other end. They walked toward it. "You know, after you," Nick said, motioning for her to open the door. "You're the cop."

Judy slowly pushed the door open to **reveal** a room with **shiny**, modern new medical equipment. They **cautious**ly walked in and looked around.

Nick pointed to **scratch**es **crisscross**ing the floor. "**Claw** marks?" Judy said, **taking in** the **sight**. There were deep **groove**s in the door, too.

Feeling a little **scared** and **intimidated**, Nick started to back up. "Yeah, huge, huge claw marks. But what kind of anima—" A **growl interrupt**ed him, and then a **lock**ed-up, **savage** tiger grabbed Nick and pulled him toward his **cell**. Judy **yank**ed Nick away, freeing him from the tiger's **grip**.

Judy held up her **flashlight** and **swivel**ed it around the room to reveal . . . **dozen**s of eyes! They walked along looking at each of the locked-up animals before finding a jaguar on all fours, **pacing** his cell. "Mr. Manchas," said Judy.

They continued past three, four, five cells, until finally,

in the last one, they found a **feral** otter. It was Emmitt Otterton!

"It's him," said Judy. "We found our otter." She turned and spoke to him gently. "Mr. Otterton, my name is Officer Judy Hopps. Your wife sent me to find you. We're gonna get you out of here now."

Otterton **screech**ed and **lunge**d toward the glass wall, as if trying to attack.

"Or not," said Nick, backing away. "Guess he's in no **rush** to get home to the Mrs."

Judy looked down the corridor of cells, counting, "Eleven, twelve, thirteen, fourteen. Plus Manchas." She thought for a moment, then said, "Chief Bogo handed out fourteen missing mammal files. . . . All the missing mammals are right here!"

*Click!* A door started to open, so Nick and Judy quickly hid next to an empty cell. They heard **footstep**s approaching, and soon they could see someone. . . .

It was Mayor Lionheart!

"Enough!" said Lionheart. "I don't want excuses, Doctor, I want answers."

Lionheart looked serious, **intense**, and tired. Judy **whip**ped out her phone and started recording as Lionheart talked to a badger* doctor.

"Mayor Lionheart, please," said the doctor. "We're doing everything we can."

"Oh, I don't think you are," said Lionheart. "Because I got a dozen and a half animals here who've **gone off-the-freaking-rails**＊ crazy, and you can't tell me why. I'd call that *awfully* far from *doing everything*."

"Sir, it may be time to consider their **biology**," said the doctor.

Otterton, in the **cage** behind them, slammed against the glass walls of his cell.

"Biology, Doctor? **Spare** me."

"We both know what they all have in common. We can't keep it a secret. We need to **come forward**," the doctor said.

Lionheart **snarl**ed and turned on the doctor. "What do

---

★ badger 오소리. 굴을 파서 사는 족제빗과 육식동물로, 앞다리가 크고 강하며 발에는 큰 발톱이 있어 땅굴 파기에 알맞다.
＊ freaking '빌어먹을'이라는 뜻의 'fucking'을 완곡하게 표현한 말.

you think will happen if the press **gets ahold of** this?"

"What does Chief Bogo think?" asked the doctor.

"Chief Bogo doesn't know. And we are going to keep it that way."

*Brrring! Brrring!* Judy's phone broke the silence. It was her parents calling.

Lionheart looked up, **startled**. "Someone's here!"

"Sir, you need to go now," said the doctor. "**Security, sweep** the area!"

Nick and Judy ran as an **alarm blare**d throughout the asylum. Wolves **swarm**ed the halls.

"Great, we're dead. That's it. I'm dead. You're dead. Everybody's dead," Nick **declare**d.

"Can you swim?" Judy asked Nick, **duck**ing into an empty cell and putting her phone into an **evidence** bag.

"What? Can I swim? Of course. Why?" Nick watched Judy **dive** into a large hippo toilet. He closed his eyes and jumped in after her.

They slid through the pipe, **twist**ing this way and that until they finally shot out, **cascading** over a waterfall. After a **gasp** of air, Nick swam to the **riverbank**. But Judy was nowhere to be seen. "Carrots? Hopps? Judy!"

He **sighed** when he saw her emerge from the water, holding her bagged phone over her head. "We've got to tell Bogo."

An hour later, the ZPD **burst** into Lionheart's office.

"Mayor Lionheart, you are under **arrest** for the **kidnap**ping and false **imprison**ment of **innocent** citizens," Judy said as she **cuff**ed him.

"You don't understand!" shouted Lionheart. "I had to do it!"

"You have the right to remain silent," Judy continued.

"I did it for the city!" Lionheart **exclaim**ed.

Later on, Bogo **address**ed the press. Behind him were posters of the savage animals—each one of them **sport**ing a **muzzle**. "Ladies and gentle**mammal**s," said Bogo. "Fourteen mammals went missing, and all fourteen have been found by our newest **recruit**, who will speak to you in a moment."

"I am so nervous," said Judy as she and Nick stood off to the side.

"Okay, Press **Conference** 101,★" said Nick. "You wanna look smart, answer their questions with your own **rhetorical** questions. Then answer that question. Okay like this, 'Was this a tough case? Yes. Yes, it was.' "

"You should be up there with me. We did this together," said Judy.

"Well, am I a cop? No. No, I'm not," answered Nick.

"Funny you should say that . . . because I've been thinking. It would be nice to have a partner," said Judy, handing Nick an **application** to the ZPD. She offered the carrot pen to him. "Here. **In case** you need something to write with."

Bellwether **gestured** to Judy to come up to the **podium**. "Officer Hopps, it's time."

Nick looked down at the application, **click**ed the pen, and began **fill**ing it **out**.

---

★101 과목 또는 강의명 뒤에 붙어서 어떤 과목의 입문과정임을 나타내는 단어로, 어떤 주제에 대한 기초 지식을 의미한다.

As Judy stepped up, Bogo **salute**d her. She saluted back, and then the reporters started shouting out her name and asking questions. Judy pointed to one of them. "What can you tell us about the animals that went savage?" the reporter asked.

"Well, the animals in question . . . Are they all different **species**? Yes. Yes, they are," said Judy, looking toward Nick.

Nick smiled and gave her a **thumbs-up.**

"Okay, what's the connection?" shouted another reporter.

"All we know is that they're all members of the **predator family**," said Judy.

Nick **frown**ed. The press reacted. Again, they **yell**ed questions all at once. Judy was surprised.

"So predators are the only ones going savage?" demanded one reporter.

"That is **accurate**," said Judy, hesitating before she spoke. "Yes."

"Why is that happening?" yelled several reporters.

"We still don't know—"

The crowd **rumble**d with **disappointment.**

"BUT, but, but . . . it may have something to do with

biology," said Judy, surprised by the **escalating tension** in the room.

**Murmur**s **rippled** across the press and a reporter asked, "What do you mean by that?"

"A **biological component**. You know, something in their DNA," Judy said.

"In their DNA? Can you **elaborate** on that, please?"

"Yes," Judy **nod**ded, as the crowd got louder. "Thousands of years ago . . . predators survived through their **aggressive** hunting **instincts**. For whatever reason, they're **revert**ing back to their savage ways."

Her comment caused a big **hubbub**. Nick didn't like what he was hearing. Clawhauser looked up. He was feeling uncomfortable, too.

"Officer Hopps, could it happen again?" asked another reporter.

"It is possible," said Judy. "We must be **vigilant**. And we at the ZPD are prepared and are here to protect you."

The press suddenly went into an absolute **frenzy**, asking questions like "What is being done to **prevent** it?" and "Should all predators be **quarantine**d?"

Bellwether stepped up, eager to **put an end to** the questions. "Uh, thank you, Officer Hopps. Uh, no more questions."

"Oh, okay . . . but . . . I . . . didn't—" Before Judy could say another word, Bellwether **usher**ed her away.

Unsure of how she had done, Judy walked across the lobby to Nick. "That went so fast. I didn't get a chance to mention you or say anything about—"

"Oh, I think you said plenty," said Nick, **interrupt**ing her.

"What do you mean?" Judy asked, confused.

"Clearly there's a biological component," he said **sarcastic**ally, repeating her words. "These predators may be reverting back to their **primitive** savage ways." He looked at her **incredulous**ly. "Are you serious?"

"I just **state**d the facts of the case," said Judy. "I mean, it's not like a bunny could go savage."

"No, but a fox could, huh?"

"Stop it, Nick! You're not like them."

"There's a *them* now?"

"You know what I mean. You're not that kind of

predator."

Nick gestured at all the posters. "The kind that needs to be muzzled? The kind that makes you think you need to carry around fox **repellent**? Yeah, don't think I didn't **notice** that little item the first time we met."

Nick got angrier and angrier, "So, you scared of me? Think I might go **nuts**? Go savage? Think I might what. . . try to eat you?"

Nick **lunged**, like he was going to **bite** her, and she **flinched**. **Automatic**ally, she put her hand on the fox repellent.

"I knew it. Just when I thought somebody actually believed in me," Nick said calmly. Then he handed her back the application. "Probably best if you don't have a predator as a partner."

As he walked away, he took off the sticker badge, **crumple**d it up, and **toss**ed it into the **trash**.

"Nick!" Judy called after him, but he went straight out the door.

Judy had broken their friendship, and she didn't know how to fix it.

After the press **conference**, a **wedge** was driven between the animals of Zootopia, and everyone was talking about it. There were **conflicts** and **protests**. The animals began to treat one another differently.

At one protest, Judy stood in the middle of the two **opposing** sides as they argued.

"Go back to the forest, predator!" a pig yelled.

"I'm from the savanna!" shouted a beaver.

As the divide between **prey** and predators grew, it was on every news **station**.

**Pop** star Gazelle **rallied** for peace. "The Zootopia I know is better than this. We don't just **blind**ly **assign blame.**

We don't know why these attacks keep happening, but it is **irresponsible** to **label** all predators as savages. We cannot let fear divide us. Please . . . give me back the Zootopia I love."

Judy felt **exhaust**ed by all the fighting—and she also felt responsible. She rode the subway on her way into work. There she watched a mother bunny pull her child to her as a lion boarded the train, and Judy shook her head. Judy got off at the next stop and went into the hospital.

"That's not my husband," Mrs. Otterton said, as she and Judy watched Emmitt Otterton **flail** around like a madman inside a **pad**ded room.

Judy sighed, her face full of worry. But there was nothing she could do.

Even inside the ZPD lobby the news was on.

Bogo called to Judy. "Come on, Hopps. The new mayor wants to see us."

"The mayor? Why?" she asked.

"It would seem you've **arrived**," Bogo said.

As Judy followed Bogo, she saw Clawhauser packing up

his desk. "Clawhauser? What're you doing?" she asked.

"Oh, they thought it would be better if a *predator* such as myself wasn't the first face you see when you walk into the ZPD. So they're moving me to Records downstairs. By the **boiler**," he said.

Judy's **disappointment** was **evident** on her face.

"Hopps. Now!" Bogo **command**ed.

Mayor Bellwether was behind her desk in her big new **fancy** office as Bogo and Judy sat down. In front of them was a **pamphlet** with a picture of a smiling Judy that read "ZPD, Put Your Trust in Us." Judy looked at it, **confused**. "I don't understand."

"Our city is ninety percent prey, Judy," said Bellwether. "And right now, they're just really **scared**. You're a hero to them. They trust you. And so that's why **Chief** Bogo and I want you to be the public face of the ZPD."

"I'm not—I'm not a hero," said Judy sadly. "I came here to make the world a better place, but I think I broke it."

"Don't give yourself so much **credit**, Hopps," said Bogo. "The world has always been broken. That's why we need good **cop**s like you."

"**With all due respect**, sir, a good cop is supposed to **serve** and protect—help the city, not **tear** it apart," said Judy. She took off her **badge** and handed it to Bogo. "I don't **deserve** this badge."

"Hopps," said Bogo.

"Judy. This is what you've always wanted. Since you were a kid . . . you can't quit . . . ," said Bellwether.

"Thank you for the opportunity," said Judy. Then she rushed out of the office.

At her family vegetable **stand** in Bunnyburrow, Judy bagged carrots for a **customer**. "Four **dozen** carrots," she said **robotic**ally. "Have a nice day."

Stu and Bonnie approached her, **concern**ed. "Hey there, Jude—Jude the Dude, remember that one? How we doin'?" asked Stu.

"I'm fine."

"You are not fine. Your ears are **droopy**," said Bonnie.

"Why did I think I could make a difference?" Judy asked.

"Well, because you're a trier, that's why," said Stu.

"You've always been a trier," said Bonnie.

"Yeah. I tried, and I made life so much worse for so many **innocent** predators."

"Oh, not all of them, though," Stu said. "**Speak of the devil.** Right on time."

*Beep!* A **horn blare**d as a bakery truck **pull**ed **up** to the stand.

Judy's eyes **widen**ed. "Is that . . . Gideon Grey?"

The truck had a **sign** that read GIDEON GREY'S EPICUREAN BAKED **DELIGHT**S . . . MADE WITH HOPPS FAMILY FARM PRODUCE.

"Yep. It sure is," Stu **nod**ded. "We work with him now."

"He's our partner! And we'd never have considered it had you not opened our minds," said Bonnie.

"That's right," said Stu. "Gid's turned into one of the top pastry chefs* in the tri**borough**s."

The fox in question climbed out of his truck. "Gideon Grey," said Judy. "I'll be darned."

"Hey, Judy," said Gideon. "I'd like to say sorry for the way I behaved in my **youth**. I had a lot of self-**doubt**

---

★pastry chef 페이스트리 셰프. 파티시에(patissier)라고도 불리며, 오븐에 굽는 음식이나 페이스트리, 디저트 등에 대해서 책임을 지는 요리사를 말한다.

that **manifest**ed itself in the form of **unchecked rage** and **aggression**. I was a major **jerk**."

"I **know a thing or two** about being a jerk," said Judy.

"Anyhow, I brought you all these pies," said Gideon, holding them up. Kid bunnies ran across the field, **beelining** it for the pies.

"Hey, kids!" shouted Stu. "Don't run through the *Midnicampum holicithias!*"

"Now, there's a four-dollar word,★ Mr. H. My family always just called them night **howl**ers," said Gideon.

Judy's ears **prick**ed **up**. "What did you say?" she asked.

Stu gestured to the flowers growing on the **edge** of the **crop**s. "Oh, Gid's talking about those flowers, Judy. I use them to keep bugs off the produce. But I don't like the little ones going near them on **account** of your Uncle Terry."

"Yeah, Terry ate one whole when we were kids and went completely **nuts**," said Bonnie.

"He **bit** the dickens✻ out of your mother," added Stu.

---

★ four-dollar word 길고 발음하기 복잡하고, 뜻도 어려운 단어를 가리키는 표현.
✻ the dickens '이런!', '빌어먹을'이라는 뜻으로 짜증스러움이나 강조를 나타내는 속어.

"A bunny can go savage . . . ," said Judy, **putting the pieces together.**

"Savage? Well, that's a strong word," said Bonnie.

"There's a **sizable** divot★ in your arm. I'd call that savage," said Stu.

Judy stood still as the thoughts **race**d through her head. "Night howlers aren't wolves. They're flowers. The flowers are making the predators go savage. That's it. That's what I've been missing." She raced away, then turned back. "Keys! Keys! Keys! Hurry! Come on!" Stu **toss**ed her the keys to his pickup truck✻ and Judy jumped in. "Thank you, I love you, bye!"

She **peel**ed **out** and raced toward Zootopia.

---

★ divot 디벗. 잔디나 땅이 골프채에 파인 자리라는 뜻으로 여기에서는 물려서 뜯긴 자국이 남았다는 의미로 쓰였다.
✻ pickup truck 짐칸의 덮개가 없는 소형 트럭.

Judy found Nick sitting in a lawn chair* under a dark, lonely bridge.

"Night howlers aren't wolves. They're **toxic** flowers. I think someone is targeting predators **on purpose** and making them go **savage**."

"Wow," said Nick. "Isn't that interesting." He got up and walked off, but Judy followed.

"Wait, listen! I know you'll never forgive me. And I don't **blame** you. I wouldn't forgive me, either. I was **ignorant** and **irresponsible** and **small-minded**. But predators shouldn't

---

★lawn chair 야외용 접이식 의자.

suffer because of my mistakes. I have to fix this, but I can't do it without you."

Nick **sigh**ed but still refused to look at her.

"And after we're done, you can hate me, and that'll be fine, because I was a **horrible** friend and I hurt you. . . . And you can walk away knowing you were right **all along**, I really am just a **dumb** bunny."

Nick didn't respond. It was **awkward**ly quiet until, suddenly, Judy's voice played back on a recorder. "I really am just a dumb bunny. I really am just a dumb bunny."

Nick **emerge**d from the shadows, holding up her carrot pen. "**Cheer up**, Carrots. I'll let you **erase** it . . . in forty-eight hours."

Judy's eyes **well**ed up with tears. Nick shook his head. "All right, get in here."

She put her arms around Nick and hugged him tightly.

"You bunnies are so **emotional**," said Nick. "Are you just trying to steal the pen? Is that what this is? You are standing on my **tail**, though. Off, off, off."

Nick and Judy climbed into the pickup truck.

"Oh! I thought you guys only grew carrots!" said Nick,

grabbing a basket of blueberries and **pop**ping a few into his mouth. "What's the plan?"

"We're gonna follow the night howlers. Know this guy?" Judy asked, holding up a picture of Duke Weaselton, the **crook** Judy had **bust**ed in Little Rodentia for stealing flower **bulb**s.

"I know everybody," said Nick.

**J**udy and Nick found Weaselton standing on a street corner, selling random **junk**. "Anything you need . . . I got it," he called. "All your favorite movies! I got movies that haven't even been **release**d yet!" In front of him were **knock-off** movies like *Wreck-It Rhino,*★ *Wrangled,*★ and *Pig Hero 6.*★

"Well, well, look who's back in the **bootleg** business," Nick said, walking up to him.

"What's it to you, Wilde? Shouldn't you be **melt**ing

---

★Wreck-It Rhino, Wrangled, Pig Hero 6 각각 Wreck-It Ralph(주먹왕 랄프), Tangled(라푼젤), Big Hero 6(빅 히어로)를 패러디한 표현.

down a pawpsicle or something?" Weaselton **recognized** Judy. "Hey, if it isn't Flopsy* the Copsy."

"We both know those weren't **moldy** onions I caught you stealing," said Judy. "What were you going to do with those night howlers, Wezzleton?"

"It's Weaselton! Duke Weaselton. And I ain't talking, rabbit. And ain't nothing you can do to make me." He **flick**ed a **toothpick** in her face. Judy turned to Nick and smiled. She knew they had the **exact** same idea.

Not long after, polar bears held Weaselton over the icy death **pit** inside Mr. Big's place. "Ice 'im," said Mr. Big.

Weaselton screamed and **squirm**ed, trying to break free. "You dirty rat!* Why you helping her? You know she's a cop!"

Mr. Big **motion**ed for his polar bears to wait as they **dangle**d Weaselton over the pit. "And the godmother to my future granddaughter."

---

★ flopsy 애완용 토끼에게 붙이는 흔한 이름 가운데 하나.
✻ dirty rat '비열한 놈' 또는 '배반자'라는 뜻을 나타내는 표현.

Fru Fru **emerged** from the other room, **showing off** her **pregnant belly**. "I'm going to name her Judy," said Fru Fru happily.

"Aw," said Judy.

"Ice this weasel," Mr. Big ordered.

"Wait! Stop! I'll talk!" screamed Weaselton. "I stole them night howlers because I could sell them for a lot of **dough**."

"And to whom did you sell them?" asked Judy.

"A ram* named Doug. We got a **drop spot underground**. Just **watch it**. Doug ain't exactly **friendly**."

---

★ram 숫양.

Nick and Judy followed Weaselton's **instructions** and found the **drop**: an old subway car in an **abandon**ed station. They hid as two tough rams exited the car.

Once the rams were gone, Nick lifted Judy and she pushed open the window to **peek** inside. "The weasel wasn't lying," she **whisper**ed as she climbed through.

The **interior** of the car had been **transform**ed into a **greenhouse**. There were **rows** upon rows of night howlers. "Yeah, looks like old Doug's **corner**ed the market on night howlers," said Nick.

*Click!* A door opened, and Judy and Nick quickly hid under a desk. They watched as a ram wearing a **lab** coat with the name DOUG on it entered and stood over the **flowering** plants. He carefully **harvest**ed the **pollen** and produced a small blue paint ball–like **pellet** of **serum**. Nick and Judy watched in **disbelief**.

Doug's phone rang and he held it to his ear. "Yeah? What's the **mark**? Cheetah in Sahara **Square**. Got it." Doug **load**ed the pellet into his gun and **cock**ed it. A map with pictures of various animal targets was on the wall behind him. "Yeah, I know they're fast. I can hit him. Listen, I hit a **tiny** little otter through the open window of a moving car," he said.

Judy and Nick shared a look. It was suddenly clear. The map **contain**ed the images of all the missing animals. The ram must have hit them with the serum from the night howlers, turning them all savage.

"Yeah, I'll **buzz** you when it's done. Or you'll see it on the news. You know, whichever comes first."

*Bam! Bam!* The two rams **bang**ed on the door.

"Hey, Doug, open up," said one of the rams.

Doug finished his call and **let** them **in**.

*Wham!* Suddenly, Judy kicked Doug in the back,

knocking him into the rams. With them on the other side of the door, she locked it, shutting them out.

"What are you doing?" shouted Nick.

The rams surrounded the subway car and pounded on the doors from outside.

"We need to get this evidence to the ZPD," said Judy.

"Okay. Got it," said Nick, picking up the case.

"No. All of it," said Judy, smiling.

"Wait, what?" Nick said. "You're a conductor now? Listen. It would take a miracle to get this rust bucket going."

She fired up the engine of the subway car and they started to move.

"Oh, hallelujah,★" Nick said in defeat.

The train gained speed and began to race down the tracks. Nick finally allowed himself to smile.

"Mission accomplished. Would it be premature for me to do a little victory toot-toot?" Nick gestured to the train whistle.

"All right," said Judy. "One toot-toot."

---

★hallelujah 할렐루야. 기쁨이나 해방감을 표현할 때 사용하는 표현으로, 원래는 하느님을 찬양한 다는 뜻을 나타내는 말이다.

*Toot! Toot!* Nick happily blew the train whistle.

*Bam!* One of the rams **burst** into the car through the door. The train slowed down as Nick and Judy tried to push him out. Nick managed to get the door closed, but the ram continued to bang up against it.

*Bam! Bam! Bam!* The other ram appeared on the **windshield** and **headbutt**ed it. "Maybe that's just **hail**?" Nick **joke**d.

*Boom!* He finally managed to **bust** through the windshield and knocked Judy out the window! She **grab**bed on to his **horn**s as the subway car continued **chug**ging down the track.

"Speed up, Nick! Speed up!" she shouted.

"Are you crazy? There's another train coming!"

"Trust me! SPEED! UP!"

A **split second** before the trains **crash**ed into each other, Judy kicked the ram into a track-**switch lever**, and the train car they were riding in changed tracks!

Then the subway car **derail**ed, and Judy and Nick **dove** out onto a **platform**. The car **explod**ed, and all its contents, **including** the night howlers, **burn**ed **to a crisp**.

"Everything's gone. We lost it all," said Judy.

Nick held up the case containing a gun and a pellet. "Yeah," he said, "except for this."

**N**ick and Judy came up the stairs from the subway and **race**d through the empty Natural History Museum on their way to the ZPD. All around them were **statue**s and **exhibit**s telling about the history of the **evolution** of Zootopia.

"There it is!" Judy said. She could see the ZPD offices through the exit doors of the museum.

"Judy! Judy!" a voice called.

They stopped and turned to see Bellwether standing behind them with two sheep **cop**s.

"**Mayor** Bellwether!" Judy said. "We found out what's happening. Someone's **dart**ing **predator**s with a **serum**— that's what's making them go savage."

"I am so proud of you, Judy. You did such a super job," said Bellwether, **applaud**ing.

"Thank you, ma'am. . . . How did you know where to find us?" asked Judy.

"I'll go ahead and take that case now," said Bellwether.

Something about the way Bellwether was acting made Judy **suspicious**. "You know what? I think Nick and I will just take this to the ZPD. . . ."

Judy turned to go, but the sheep **block**ed their way. Why wouldn't Bellwether let them leave? **All of a sudden,** it became **crystal clear** to Judy. Bellwether was the one behind this from the very beginning! That was why she had known where they would be. Judy **signal**ed to Nick and they **dash**ed off down a **corridor** as Bellwether shouted, "Get them!"

While she and Nick were running as fast as they could toward the police department, Judy **glance**d over her shoulder. She didn't see the woolly mammoth* **tusk** sticking out in front of her, and ran right into it. Judy

---

★woolly mammoth 털매머드. 약 480만 년 전부터 4000년 전까지 존재했던 포유류로 혹심한 추위에도 견딜 수 있게 온몸이 털로 뒤덮여 있었지만, 마지막 빙하기 때 멸종한 것으로 추정된다.

screamed in pain as the tusk **slash**ed her leg and **knock**ed her off her feet.

"Carrots!" shouted Nick.

Nick **rush**ed to her. Her leg was **bleed**ing badly. He carried her behind a **pillar**. "I got you, come here. Okay, but just relax." A few blueberries rolled out from Nick's pocket. "Blueberry?" he asked, offering one to Judy.

"Pass," she said.

"Come on out, Judy!" called Bellwether.

"Take the case," Judy **whisper**ed passing it to Nick. "Get it to Bogo."

"I'm not going to leave you behind. That's not happening," said Nick.

"I can't walk," said Judy.

"Just . . . we'll think of something," said Nick.

"We're on the same team, Judy!" said Bellwether, trying to get Judy to **surrender**. "**Underestimate**d. **Underappreciated**," she went on. "Aren't you sick of it? Predators—they may be strong and loud, but **prey outnumber** predators ten to one. Think about it: ninety percent of the **population, unite**d against a common enemy.

We'll be **unstoppable**."

Bellwether **spot**ted the shadow of long rabbit ears against the wall and **gesture**d to the sheep. They **pounce**d, but it was just a **mummified** jackalope.★ Judy and Nick **made a run for it.**

"Over there!" Bellwether shouted.

*Whack!* A sheep **tackle**d them, knocking the case out of Nick's **grip** and sending them both into a **sunken** diorama.✳ Bellwether looked over the **edge** from above.

"What are you going to do?" asked Judy. "Kill me?"

"Of course not . . . *he* is," said Bellwether, gesturing to Nick. She took the dart gun out of the case and aimed at Nick. *Thwick!* The dart sank into Nick's skin.

"No! Nick!" Judy **yell**ed.

Nick started to shake and **crouch**ed over as Bellwether **dial**ed her phone.

"Yes, police!" Bellwether said into the phone. "There's a savage fox in the Natural History Museum. **Officer** Hopps

---

★jackalope jackrabbit(산토끼)와 antelope(영양)의 합성어로 토끼의 몸에 영양의 뿔이 달린 상상 속의 동물이다.

✳diorama 디오라마. 여러 모형을 배경과 함께 설치하여 특정 장면을 구성한 전시품.

is down! Please hurry!"

Judy searched for a way out of the diorama, but there was nowhere to go. Nick, now on all fours, looked like a wild animal. "No. Nick," said Judy. "Don't do this. Fight it."

"Oh, but he can't help it, can he?" said Bellwether. "Since preds are just *biologically* predisposed to be savages."

Nick **stalk**ed Judy like a predator about to attack as she **helpless**ly tried to **limp** away.

"**Gosh**, think of the **headline**: 'Hero Cop Killed by Savage Fox,'" said Bellwether, **pleased** with herself.

"So that's it? Prey fears predator, and you stay in power?" asked Judy.

"Pretty much," said Bellwether.

"It won't work," said Judy.

"Fear always works," said Bellwether. "And I'll dart every predator in Zootopia to keep it that way."

Nick **growl**ed as he **corner**ed Judy.

"Bye-bye, bunny," said Bellwether.

Nick **lunge**d at Judy. Bellwether smiled.

"Blood, blood, blood!" shouted Judy. "And death."

Bellwether looked on, completely **confused**.

Nick stood up and helped Judy to her feet.

"All right, you know, you're **milk**ing it. Besides, I think we got it, I think we got it. We got it up there, thank you, yakety yak*—you **laid** it all **out** beautifully," Nick said.

"What?" Bellwether said, trying to **figure out** what was going on.

Nick held up the ball of serum, then gestured to the gun. "Yeah," he said. "Oh, are you looking for the serum? Well, it's right here."

"What you've got in the **weapon** there—those are blueberries. From my family's farm," said Judy.

"They are delicious. You should try some."

Nick **lick**ed his fingers.

Bellwether looked down to see a blueberry in the **chamber** of the dart gun.

"I **framed** Lionheart, I can frame you! It's my word against yours!" she yelled angrily.

Nick held the carrot pen up high into the air so that

---

★ yakety yak '수다', '재잘거림' 또는 '허튼소리'라는 뜻의 속어.

Bellwether could see it.

"Oh, yeah, actually . . . ," Judy started.

Nick pressed a button on the pen, and Bellwether's voice played back: "And I'll dart every predator in Zootopia to keep it that way. . . ."

". . . it's your word against yours," said Judy.

Judy and Nick looked at one another and smiled. "It's called a hustle, sweetheart," they said together.

**27**

The next day, all the news **channel**s aired **footage** of Bellwether in an orange jumpsuit,★ being led to **jail**.

"Former **mayor** Dawn Bellwether **is behind bars** today, **guilty** of **mastermind**ing the **savage** attacks that have **plague**d Zootopia of late," said a **newscaster**.

The footage showed Lionheart being led *out* of **prison**.

"Her **predecessor**, Leodore Lionheart, denies any knowledge of her **plot**, claiming he was just trying to protect the city," the newscaster said. "A reporter interviewed Lionheart from jail."

---

★jumpsuit 점프수트. 바지와 상의가 하나로 붙어있는 옷이나 작업복을 가리킨다. orange jumpsuit 는 일반적으로 교도소에 수감된 재소자가 입는 옷을 말한다.

"Did I falsely **imprison** those animals? Well, yes. Yes, I did. Classic 'doing the wrong thing for the right reason' **scenario**. Know what I mean, Kitty?"

"No. No, I do not," answered the reporter, **deadpan**.

Back in the studio, the newscaster continued. "In related news, doctors say the night **howl**er **antivenom** is proving **effective** in **rehabilitating** all of the **victim**s."

When Mr. Otterton awoke inside the hospital, his wife was hugging him tightly. Judy was there, watching and smiling.

"Thank you," said Mrs. Otterton **gratefull**y.

Months later, Judy stood proudly at a **lectern** giving the **commencement address** to **graduate**s of the Zootopia Police Academy.

"When I was a kid, I thought Zootopia was this perfect place where everyone **got along** and anyone could be anything. . . . Turns out, real life's a little bit more **complicated** than a **slogan** on a bumper sticker.* Real life is **messy**. We all have **limitations**. We all make mistakes,

---

★bumper sticker 자동차의 범퍼에 붙이는 구호나 표어 등이 적힌 스티커.

which means . . . hey, glass half full! We all have a lot in common. And the more we try to understand one another, the more **exceptional** each of us will be. But we have to try. No matter what type of animal you are, from the biggest elephant to our first fox, I **implore** you: Try. Try to make a difference. Try to make the world better. Try to look inside yourself and **recognize** that change starts with you. It starts with me. It starts with all of us."

Nick approached the stage. He stood tall in front of her, his chest out. Judy **pin**ned on his **badge**.

The crowd went wild with **applause** as **cadet**s threw their caps high up into the air.

"All right! Enough! Shut it!" said **Chief** Bogo.

Judy and Nick took their seats among the other **cop**s in the bullpen. Bogo stood up at the front, calling order. "We have some new **recruit**s with us this morning," said Bogo. "**Including** our first fox. But . . . who cares?"

"You should have your own **line** of **inspirational greet**ing cards, sir," said Nick **sarcastic**ally.

"Shut your mouth, Wilde," said Bogo, then began calling out **assign**ments. When he finally got to Judy and Nick, they waited eagerly. "Hopps, Wilde . . . Skunk Pride **Parade. Dismiss**ed."

"Fun," said Nick. "Funny guy."

"Parade **detail** is a step up from parking duty," Judy said.

Bogo looked as if he was going to smile . . . but then he didn't.

**"S**o are all rabbits bad drivers, or is it just you?" asked Nick.

Judy **slam**med on the brakes, causing Nick to **lurch** forward, **accidental**ly **jam**ming his pawpsicle into his face.

"Oops. Sorry," she said.

"**Sly** bunny," said Nick, **wiping** his face.

"**Dumb** fox."

"Come on, you know I love you," said Nick.

"Do I know that? Yes. Yes, I do."

Judy and Nick smiled at each other. Suddenly, a **tricked-out** red sports car **blast**ed past them going over a hundred miles per hour. Their smiles got even wider, and Nick hit the **siren**. *Bwoop! Bwoop!* Judy **stomp**ed on the gas and they **took off, chasing** after the sports car, **catch**ing **air** along the way.